Brad Kauzlaric

The Life & Works of a Pacific Northwest Artist

Clayton Kauzlaric

Foreword by Deloris Tarzan Ament
Afterword by DeAnna Kauzlaric Kieffer
Edited by Christine Clifton-Thornton

Copyright 2014 Clayton Kauzlaric & The Kauzlaric Art Trust

Images copyright 2014 The Kauzlaric Art Trust except where otherwise noted
Printed in the USA by Lightning Source International
Published by Beep Games, Inc.
Woodinville, Washington USA
ISBN: 978-0-9899682-2-5
Library of Congress Control Number: 2014906229

First printed 2014
Paperback Edition 2025

Cover design by Clayton Kauzlaric—cover photo by DeAnna Kauzlaric Kieffer
Manufactured in the United States of America
Cover artwork: *The Foolish Virgins*, oil on Masonite, 1980
Back cover artwork: *September 34th, Shrimp Pot, Children of the Moon*

Contents

Foreword	1
Introduction	3
Biographical Sketch	8
Early Works	54
Paintings	58
Still Life	62
Surrealism	80
The Trees Series	104
Portraits	116
Mosaics	125
Devotional Work	149
Buildings & Landscapes	167
Sculpture & Other Media	180
Unfinished Works	191
Missing Works	204
Afterword by DeAnna Kauzlaric Kieffer	211

Enter ye,

Single-y,

Or in a merry band,

With lies upon your smiling lips,

And money in your hand.

Brad Kauzlaric – 1970s

Thinking About Brad

With each passing year, it becomes more clear to me that the most painful part of aging is not physical infirmity. It is the steady, often silent, disappearance of someone from among my earliest and dearest friends and family. They die. Mother. Father. Brothers and sisters. No pictures or letters can compensate for the loss of ability to touch a loved hand, or be half of a warm hug.

Brad Kauzlaric fits into a too-soon-departed friends niche in my life. So it is a special pleasure to behold his presence in these pages written by his son and his widow, and to know that he and his story soon will be available in book form.

We can be certain of nothing about death, except our feelings. My feeling about Brad is that whatever niche of heaven he occupies is brightened by his knowledge that in death, he is celebrated as an artist – as he long wished to be in life.

Although for more than 20 years I was the art critic for *The Seattle Times* and Brad was an artist, I did not meet him in the course of his art. My job in the Features Department of *The Seattle Times* included writing feature stories on a variety of topics. One such story—the one that led to meeting Brad—was a section page devoted to hunting wild mushrooms, my long-term hobby.

The Pacific Northwest is blessed with a wide range of edible mushroom delicacies, some abundant, others scarce. One of the first things I learned was the importance of being able to identify each variety, and distinguish the good from the possibly toxic – of which there are many. I armed myself with *The Mushroom Hunter's Field Guide*, by Alexander H. Smith, a practical guide to hunting and identifying mushrooms, published in 1958 by the University of Michigan Press. My copy is a 1964 second printing.

The story that caught Brad's attention dealt with the joy of returning home from a hunt one Sunday afternoon with 18 pounds of edible mushrooms, many of them morels, a choice spring variety. I have never seen a commercial version of morels.

A few days after the story appeared, I returned to my desk from a field trip to visit several art galleries that had new exhibitions for which I would write reviews. I was startled to find my desk covered with a load of fresh mushrooms. An accompanying note bore the name and phone number of Brad Kauzlaric. I couldn't remember ever having heard of him, much less having met him. But I'm a fool for wild mushrooms.

Within the hour, I called Brad's number to thank him for the bounty he'd brought in and placed in the hands of a copy aide to deliver to my desk. We had a long conversation. It is a code among mushroom hunters that one would sooner sell his firstborn than divulge the location of a rich lode of fine specimens. So Brad did not say where he'd found the mushrooms he'd brought in, merely that he found many of them each year, so his location was a treasure indeed.

Then something remarkable occurred. Brad invited my husband and me to visit him on the weekend ahead, at his home in Seabeck, on the Olympic Peninsula. He wanted to take us to one of his favorite mushroom-hunting grounds, near his home. I was like a kid in a candy store. I knew before I saw the first of his roadside finds that I would forthwith be a keeper of his secret locations. I could not repay Brad's generosity by telling others of his spots.

Mushrooms were not the only discoveries that day. We had the great pleasure of meeting DeAnna, Brad's warm and charming wife, whom we have come to treasure more each time we are in her company. Happily, that first excursion was such a success that we received annual renewals of the invitation for the next few years. Sadly, Brad has gone on to hunting grounds where we cannot join him for as long as we live.

I never wrote about Brad's art, for the same reason I never wrote critical reviews about work by other artists who were my friends. I could not be impartial.

A few weeks after our initial visit, I was surprised to be asked whether I would consent to sit for Brad to paint my portrait. It was an education to model for an artist who took his work as seriously as Brad did. Like many other noted artists of his generation (Mark Tobey, Morris Graves, Guy Anderson), Brad's work included heavy use of black and other dark tones. It has been supposed that such use of black reflects the long-time influence of Asian artists in the Northwest, whose work derives drama from the inclusion of sumi-e ink among the media.

Brad's portrait of me – slightly larger than life – showed me in a black dress, looking somber. Sadly, that painting is among his missing works. We trust its absence is temporary. The search for it continues.

Brad had the heart of an artist. His immersion in the beauty of the Northwest landscape was a hot button for many of his artworks. He was classically trained, and liked to let his art do the talking. Let us trust the Northwest will yield many of his "lost" artworks, and the presence of this book will prompt many people who own or know the location of some of the "lost" artworks to contact Clayton, Brad's son, and offer photographs which will pave the way to a wide and lasting recognition of Brad's art.

Deloris Tarzan Ament, 2014

Introduction

My dad was an artist.

One of my first memories is of Dad working in his studio. No matter where we lived, a good chunk of our home's square footage was devoted to his artistic pursuits. But Dad had a day job. His workplaces varied in his younger days, but he eventually settled at the local sanitation company and worked there for over thirty years.

I always thought of Dad's vocation and his calling as two separate things. I think he did, too. In his darker moments he groused about his lot in life. It was natural to think of his job as some sort of dead end for an artistic soul. It was only after he died in 2007 that I started thinking about his career differently. Collecting images for this book gave me perspective I never had while Dad was alive. He took one of the world's hardest jobs and made it part of his creative process. Many of the images in this book wouldn't exist if he hadn't been a garbage man.

He never spoke much about his process, or how he incorporated locations, objects, and people he encountered into his art. His keen appreciation for vanishing architecture and the fragile natural beauty of the Pacific Northwest are vividly portrayed in many of his paintings and mosaics. Locations featured in his paintings are often places he passed as he worked his route. Objects in many of his still life paintings were salvaged

Introduction

from the garbage cans of Kitsap County residents. Some of the texture in his mosaics is from bits of broken glass, or shells he collected from local beaches he passed while driving his truck. His job put him out in the world where he could observe people, places, and moments of unexpected beauty. These all appear in his artwork.

In his later years, Dad was free of his sanitation job. Once my siblings and I were out of the house and he retired he was more free to pursue art full time. He briefly operated a gallery in Seabeck, Washington, in 1997. He enjoyed socializing with other artists and the people down at Seabeck Landing, but he wasn't really suited to that as a vocation.

The fact is, my dad's creative peak was during the 1970s and 80s, when he was emptying hundreds of garbage cans a day. He was amazingly prolific during that period, given the demands on his time and energy. Looking at the span

Kitsap Sun, Bremerton, Wash., used by permission.

The only known picture of Brad Kauzlaric (left) at his disposal job. A load caught fire in 1978, forcing him to dump it in the middle of a a road near Bremerton.

of his creative output, it seems as if he lost some focus and clarity once he no longer had the contact with the world that his job provided.

My father's art covered a wide range of subject matter over sixty years. His interests were varied, as were the materials he used to express his ideas. But there are themes that appear consistently throughout his body of work.

Subjects related to nature were a consistent favorite. Though he gave up studying engineering in favor of art his first year in college, he always looked at nature with a deep appreciation for its designs and the superb functionality of its forms. He was endlessly fascinated by sea creatures, trees, and plant life. His mosaics of marine life are precise, meticulously detailed images. This clarity and precision was even more pronounced in his still life paintings. The patina on rusted farm equipment or the way an old bottle bends light were captured with an uncompromising, crisp, yet energetic style.

Categorizing Dad's body of work is a challenge. He was a surrealist, a realist, a mosaicist—but he didn't ascribe to an established school or a single style. He dabbled with abstract art in college, but didn't inhale. In fact, he professed a strong dislike for abstract art by the 1960s. Something about its unstructured, subjective nature seemed to bother him. It was his belief that his work would find an audience one day based on its merits, not on emulating trends in the art world. Dad adhered to classical techniques and was always interested in the engineering aspects that underlie art, whether it pertained to prepping a canvas or defining the lighting and perspective of an imaginary vista.

It's telling that a large percentage of Dad's works ended up in the hands of family and friends. Dad genuinely liked people, but he couldn't tolerate overt slickness or salesmanship. Dad was all too willing to cut a deal when he liked somebody. He always put people and friendship ahead of financial gain.

Dad liked the idea of being a full-time, professional artist, but he spent most of his life convinced he didn't want to associate with other artists. When I showed an interest in pursuing art, he cautioned me about other artists. He expressed his opinions in competitive terms and seemed to believe in an "us or them" mentality. He cautioned against interacting with other artists, claiming it was

Introduction

necessary to "stand on their heads" to succeed. He also seemed concerned that other artists might steal his ideas. I don't know if his experiences supported this point of view, or whether it was an excuse to remain disengaged from the larger world of the arts. Only in his later years did he come to understand the immense pleasure of associating with other artists. Without this shift in his thinking, I doubt he would have gained the mindset to open his gallery in Seabeck.

This book is light on interpretations of the artwork itself. Dad preferred to let his work do the talking. He didn't follow trends or movements in the art world. He wasn't terribly interested in the work of his contemporaries, unless they were actual friends. He was a classically trained, traditional artist with little regard for the idea of a target audience or critical praise. He also disliked talking about the meaning of artwork—his or anyone else's. Dad felt that meaning shouldn't be given up so easily or without some investment of time and attention by both the artist and the viewer.

When I started working on this book, my original plan was to assemble Dad's complete works. I came close, as I scoured the Puget Sound region with my trusty Olympus E-310. But some pieces simply fell through the cracks. I've tried to include a record of these works (see *Missing Works*, p. 204), though the quality of some images is sometimes extremely poor since only old, blurry Polaroid photos are all I could find for some pieces. My hope is that more pieces will resurface in time and join the rest of the book in future revisions. There are gaps in the narrative of this volume, too. It tends to focus more heavily on Dad's younger days and when he was most active as an artist. My mother and I did our best to make the biography comprehensive, but I simply didn't see him as much once I no longer lived in Kitsap County.

This volume contains the bulk of Brad Kauzlaric's lifetime output as an artist and hopefully conveys something about the people and places that shaped his work. An artist who lives by his craft often learns how to please an audience, or his clients. It's a basic law of survival. Dad never had that pressure. Consequently, there are works that stand out more than others in terms of quality and execution. Some are brilliant. Others are perhaps a bit self-indulgent. But there is no denying the passion and energy that went into their creation. The farm boy from Wisconsin adopted Washington State as his true home, and the affection

Introduction

he had for its places, people, and nature are abundantly clear on many of these pages.

This book wouldn't be complete without acknowledging the gracious people who opened their doors and memories to help make this retrospective possible, from family to friends and complete strangers. As I traveled around the Puget Sound region, visiting homes and photographing art, I was grateful for a chance to see my dad the way others saw him. I'd also like to thank my friend Pat Hoynes for helping out with gear, lighting, and some camera work, particularly when we photographed the massive collection of artwork at my parent's house.

I'm told it gets hard to remember how a loved one looked or sounded after they're gone. That's not remotely possible with Dad. Between his strong personality, booming voice, and distinctive appearance, he always made a lasting impression. I hope this record will serve as a reminder of who he was for those who knew him and an introduction for those who are just getting acquainted. The works in this book are a testament to his creativity and boundless curiosity about the world around him.

Clayton Kauzlaric, 2014

Biographical Sketch

The Old Country

Brad Kauzlaric's parents, Jake and Catherine, were both of Croatian descent. His grandparents arrived in the United States between the late 1890s and early 1900s from various parts of Croatia, which was then still part of the Austro–Hungarian empire. Many of Brad's aunts and uncles were born in Europe, though both of his parents were from a younger set born in the United States after their families arrived.

His grandfather Valentine Kauzlaric came from the mountainous area near Mrkopalj, Croatia, in 1900 when he was 21 years old, at first joining other family members to work in coal mines near Centerville, Iowa. There, he married Helen Raski in 1901. One day, Valentine read an article in a Croatian language newspaper about opportunities in northeastern Wisconsin. Eager to leave the mines, he moved to the Eagle River vicinity and took up farming. Once he was established, he bought into a brownstone-making business. Later, he added to his collection

Brad's mother, Catherine "Kay" Kauzlaric, outside the family home in Eagle River, Wisconsin, 1935. Brad was born in the house one year later.

of businesses when he built and operated the Aerio Tavern on Highway 45. He and Helen had ten children—five boys and five girls. Brad's father, Jacob "Jake" Kauzlaric, was their fifth child, born in 1910.

Jake's family remembered Valentine as a shrewd businessman with piercing blue eyes who expected his children to either work on the farm or at the tavern. If they worked elsewhere, they were expected to turn over their paychecks to him as long as they lived under his roof.

Kauzlaric's maternal grandfather, Mato "Matthew" Scorich, came to America in 1908. Even though Matthew said he loved America "at first sight," he thought of himself as a visitor to the United States rather than an immigrant. He had planned to return to Croatia one day but his wife, Marija, would have

Kauzlaric's grandparents, Helen and Valentine Kauzlaric (far right), *at the family home in Centerville, Iowa, in 1915.*

Biographical Sketch

none of it. Matthew could never leave his children, but, like many immigrants, sadness would settle over him when he thought of his boyhood home. Among the children he had with Mary was Kaija/Catherine "Kay" Scorich, born in 1915.

Catherine was an identical twin and shared a typically close bond with her sister, Marie. They grew up with eight brothers and sisters. Their mother, Marija, was remembered as a strong, no-nonsense personality who took charge of her brood and her mild-mannered husband as well.

When Catherine was asked why her generation knew so little about the old country, she said, "My parents and others left so much behind—their families, their homeland. When my mother said goodbye to my grandfather in Trieste to join her first husband in America, it was after an 80-mile ride in a cart pulled by oxen. She knew she would never see her father again. In those years, communication was limited. It was very expensive to send a letter to America. If a letter did arrive, it usually meant someone had died." Catherine also emphasized that her parents were

Top: *Twin daughters Kaija (Catherine) and Maia (Marie) accompanied by their godparents, 1917.*

Bottom,: *Kaija "Kay" and Maia's first communion, 1923.*

determined to be good United States citizens—to shed their old identities and build new lives. Even though both of Brad's parents spoke Croatian, they avoided transmitting the language to him and his brother, Gary.

Between their large garden, frugal habits, and enterprising spirit, the Scorich family survived the ups and downs of the Chisholm, Minnesota, economy that relied on mining in the Mesabi Iron Range. Later, his grandchildren would remember Grandpa Mato sitting in his garden in his rocker—a favorite spot. One day, he overheard the women talking about a new grandson named Bradley. He turned to one of them and asked, "Who ees dis Ba-rah-dley?" This little story was passed along, not because Grandpa asked the question in broken English, but because all the other children had "real" names like Joseph, Peter, Dan, and the like.

After Mato died in a mine-related accident in 1947, Marija continued to live in Chisholm, where the scent of windowsill geraniums filled her kitchen on winter days as she knitted slippers for dozens of grandchildren.

Top: *Brad's mother Kay in 1928.*

Bottom: *His father Jake in 1930.*

Biographical Sketch

The Summer People

Eagle River, Wisconsin, was a popular getaway for well-heeled Midwestern families. Industrialist Charles Ray Whitney, his wife Zola, and his sister Ethel had a summer home in the area situated on several manicured acres.

The Whitneys befriended an outgoing and likeable local, Jake Kauzlaric, and included him in their circle of friends when staying at their craftsman-style home. Jake's mother, Helen, died when he was still a teenager in 1927. Jake enjoyed the attention and the advantages offered by these cultured, affluent people. He worked for and socialized with them. Being childless, they welcomed him into their lives in an expansive manner. This included paying for his tuition at agricultural college.

Valentine may have resented the relationship between his son and his benefactors. He reportedly refused an offer by the Whitneys to adopt Jake and other offers to support him. Consequently, Jake lived between two worlds—a mindset that came between him and his wife more than once in the years ahead. Even after his marriage to Catherine Scorich, they lived on the fringe of the lives of the "summer people" in

Left to right: *Kay & Jake Kauzlaric, infant Bradley Kauzlaric, Ethel Whitney, and Ray Whitney, 1937.*

Eagle River, enjoying picnics, boating, and dinners as well as the company of artists and authors—yet they were not really a part of that life.

Farm Life

Catherine married Jake in 1935. Their first son, Bradley, was born on February 5, 1936. Brad arrived during a Wisconsin snowstorm. Fortunately, the local physician and his nurse were able to reach Catherine and Jake's small farmhouse before the storm arrived in full force, which stranded them there. "My doctor and husband drank coffee and played cards while I paced the floor," Brad Kauzlaric's mother, Catherine, would later say, describing the long labor of her first child.

In 1938, with freezing temperatures outside again and Brad's younger brother Gary on the way, Catherine taught young Brad to read to keep him busy, using a McGuffey Reader, a staple of schoolhouses across America at the time. Reading opened a world of ideas

Charles "Ray" Whitney (1879–1954) was a prominent maritime lawyer and industrialist. He was president and chairman of the Lake Torpedo Boat Company in Bridgeport, Connecticut, and of the California Shipbuilding Company in Longbeach, California. His companies built many of America's submarines during World War I. Ray and Zola's house remains a landmark in Waukegan, Illinois.

Above, left to right: *Zola Whitney, Ambassador Fred Whitney, Charles "Ray" Whitney*

Right: *Kay Kauzlaric & Brad on the Whitney's boat, 1939.*

Biographical Sketch

Zola Whitney in 1939. Ray Whitney was an avid amateur photographer. He shot and developed many of the photos of the Kauzlaric family on these pages.

and different cultures to him, and became a lifelong passion. He soon read everything in sight and entertained older cousins by reading the Sunday comics to them.

On summer days, his father, Jake, a talented raconteur, would occasionally invite neighboring children to enjoy the books and stories he shared with Brad and Gary. Brad's parents worked diligently to give him an educational foundation, but his adventures in fields and woods were equally informative. Always a keen observer, Brad delighted in watching and learning about bugs, butterflies, birds, and animals. He clearly enjoyed learning about the talents of local snapping turtles thanks to a demonstration his father gave him using a broomstick.

As unofficial grandparents, the Whitneys indulged the Kauzlaric boys with an abundance of books, clothes, and toys. These things set them apart from other family members. These tokens of affection slowly became a source of frustration and resentment. With his farm struggling and debts piling up, Jake decided to move away from Eagle River. Catherine thought it was for the best.

For a time, they owned a floral shop in Antigo, Wisconsin. This was one of the few places Brad remembered with fondness. After that, a pattern emerged, with Jake continuously moving his family from one place to another, seeking the success that may have once seemed so close while living near the Whitneys and their friends.

Heading West

It's possible that the ever-changing locales and shifting fortunes of the Kauzlarics had an effect on Brad's development as an artist. Permanence and change would become a common theme in many works he created later in life. This was expressed through subjects grounded in nature, but also included frequent use of derelict buildings, broken objects that were once whole, and trees in autumn and spring—two seasons of greatest change.

Jake and Catherine worked hard to improve their lives. His father continued looking for bigger and better opportunities. The family sometimes moved to places lacking electricity or indoor plumbing. Brad later remembered how Catherine cleaned and scrubbed tirelessly to make these places suitable for her family. His father would improve farm buildings, fix equipment, and barter for supplies and stock. When they grew older, the boys had plenty of chores that included chopping firewood, helping in the family garden, and feeding chickens and other animals.

Once Brad started attending public school, a teacher suggested that he skip a couple of grades. After

Top: *Brad Kauzlaric and younger brother Gary at the family farm in Eagle River, Wisconsin, 1941.*

Bottom: *The boys the same year visiting the Whitney's summer home.*

consulting Catherine's half-brother, a teacher named John Jurkovich, his parents did not advance him. Brad was small for his age, and they saw this as another disadvantage in addition to a common reluctance to skip grades at that time. During the family's many moves, he attended at least a dozen grade schools, many of them one-room schools, where he was bored with his lessons. Instead, he liked to listen to the teachers present lessons to the upper-grade students. With a boyish cheekiness, he didn't hesitate to correct anyone if they mispronounced a word or presented a fact in error. This habit did not endear him to some teachers.

Brad's early years in Wisconsin, where his parents farmed, raised vegetables and chickens, were the kind that build character and resiliency. To augment their income, Jacob worked as a model for newspaper and magazine advertisements in Waukegan during the winter months. Jake was a handsome man with a refined manner and dress that created job opportunities in this and associated careers. He appeared in a number of catalogs and newspaper advertisements through much of the 1940s.

Jake retained an abiding interest in poultry nutrition from his days at the agricultural college and remained an amateur researcher for the rest of his life. Regardless of their living space, Jacob would often brood chicks someplace and experiment with feed formulas. When he died in Seattle in 1962, he left jars of feed mixes on the stairs to the basement, each formula meticulously labeled in a code only he could decipher.

The Kauzlaric family left Wisconsin for Canyon City, Colorado, in 1948. They lived there for a year

Above: *Jake Kauzlaric* (left) *in a* Minneapolis Star *newspaper ad, 1947.*

Below: *Fifteen-year-old Brad with a fresh catch in Bremerton, Washington, 1951.*

so Catherine could spend time with her twin sister, Marie, whose husband, Harley Rice, was stationed with the army nearby at Fort Carson. Twelve-year-old Bradley liked Colorado right away. He was impressed with the area's geology and readily joined hiking excursions to explore caves and learn more about rock formations and the high desert. This contact with nature would prove a lasting part of his creative and personal interests that would remain strong the rest of his life.

Jake and Catherine moved to Washington State the following year, initially staying with relatives in Bremerton before settling in Poulsbo, on the Kitsap peninsula, where Brad attended North Kitsap Junior High School. Jake continued to try his hand at different trades and business ideas, but this would all occur in the Puget Sound region. Brad may not have known it at the time, but his days of moving from place to place were done. Brad would remain in Western Washington for the rest of his life, taking only a handful of trips outside the region. Even with family moves from Bainbridge Island to Bremerton and Poulsbo, he finally found a lasting home in the Pacific Northwest.

Early Interests

As young teens, Brad and his brother Gary were treated to trips with their aunt and uncle, Julia and Al Nelson. Only a dozen years older than Brad, Al enthusiastically showed the boys "his" Northwest. One of their favorite places to pick oysters and enjoy a bonfire was on the beach at Hood Canal in the Seabeck area. Brad imagined then that he might like to live in Seabeck one day.

Uncle Al Nelson, Brad, Gary, and Jake Kauzlaric in 1952 near Silverdale, Washington.

Biographical Sketch

Along with his brother and other boys, they spent many hours chasing the fast, elusive fish in the waterways and coves near Poulsbo. Across Liberty Bay, he was thrilled to find a Native American arrowhead that he would match to one in a Canadian museum years later. Decades later, his large mosaic, *Holy Flounder* (1999, p. 144), was inspired by the quest for flounder buried in the sandy bottom of Dogfish Creek near Front Street.

Uncle Al captured many of these trips with his camera and left a strong impression on the minds of the two young men from the Midwest. Gary would become an accomplished outdoorsman who later shared his love of nature through volunteer work in Port Angeles, Washington. Brad brought these experiences to his artwork with an appreciation of nature's images, whether in the contours of a salmon or the subtle coloring of an erupting alder bud. The pursuit of art didn't figure in Brad's life yet, at least not in a way anyone could recall during this time. In his late teens, Brad continued to explore the area with friends who liked to camp, fish, and hike the forests and waterways in Kitsap County and surrounding areas. When they weren't working part-time jobs, Brad and his friends John Berkeley, Ron Bedford, Jack Walthall, Ken Crawford, and others explored logging roads, boated the Kitsap Peninsula, and took trips to the ocean beaches. One of their favorite places was a small, hidden lake in Port Orchard that could only be approached by foot that is now part of the McCormick Woods Golf Course.

Left to right: *Kay & Jake Kauzlaric, Brad, Julia Nelson, and Gary Kauzlaric, 1952.*

Brad playing a guitar in his bedroom in Bremerton, 1954.

Art projects in progress in Brad's bedroom, 1956.

Brad took some basic flight lessons at Bremerton National Airport in his teens and briefly considered a career in the military as he graduated from high school in 1954. He enrolled at Olympic College to study engineering and signed up for a Marine Corps training program. Either his study habits or disenchantment with the program prompted a mutual parting of the ways. Brad had a lifelong difficulty with authority and eventually realized he couldn't imagine a successful outcome in a life in the armed forces.

A New World

Olympic College offered an interesting mix of opportunities. Founded just seven years earlier in 1946, the community college served local high school graduates like Brad and veterans returning from the Korean War. The campus is still located near the south end of the Warren Avenue bridge in Bremerton and at first consisted of former government buildings from World War II. As a Navy town, Bremerton was home to a varied cross-section of people from across the US and abroad.

Brad registered at first for mechanical engineering classes but included a painting class when he learned that a girl he liked was doing the same. The girl never showed up for the class, but Brad discovered a world that changed his life. At this time, his family lived just two blocks from Olympic College, so Brad could walk over to the art department anytime he liked. This was helpful given the lack of available workspace in his parents' small house.

Brad's initial interest in engineering and talent for construction would become a part of his artwork in the future. Beyond his natural eye for perspective, anatomy, and lighting, Brad would carefully construct armatures for sculptures, and build lit stages for his still life subjects. His fascination with construction techniques would later find its expression through large mosaic panels and stained glass windows framed

Biographical Sketch

Harrison Blass (lower right) *hands a tesserae tile to his student Brad Kauzlaric* (center), *1955. The mosaic,* The Progress of Man, *remained on the college science building until it was dismantled in 2008.*

with concrete. The latter were built using techniques he devised himself with the intent that they would last for generations.

His art teacher at Olympic College, Harrison "Hank" Blass, was a major influence, not in terms of style or subject matter, but in the way Blass encouraged attention to detail and the importance of mastering the fundamentals of a given medium. Blass was a classically trained painter and a skilled mosaicist, two passions he passed on to his pupil. Blass enlisted a number of his students, including Brad, to assist him during construction of a large mosaic on the exterior of the college science building. This was among Brad's first experiences with the medium, and it would share equal footing with oil painting for the rest of his life. Years later, at work in his studio, Brad would follow Blass' classical approach to art while remembering Hank's salty warnings about the pitfalls of the art world.

If there was a disadvantage to having a mentor like Blass, it was his insistence that other artists were not to be trusted, and a sense that those who lacked discipline and training were lesser artists. This view stuck with Brad for many years and may have cost him in terms of professional networking and opportunities to collaborate with other artists. Blass couldn't have known it, but this fit with Brad's family sense of being from two worlds. Even as an artist, Brad felt set apart: outside a world he desperately wanted to be a part of, just as his father was close to the Whitneys but not a part of their world.

In Hank's retirement years, he and his former student became good friends. Brad was among a handful of

old associates who kept an eye on his aging mentor and his wife, Maria. Former students helped Blass with work around the couple's house at Enetai Beach, in Bremerton. "Sketching trips" were just as often excursions to Hank's favorite eateries, where he could indulge in unhealthy food and drink beer. These times were something Brad valued. They affectionately referred to each other as "old bastards." Brad enjoyed having access to the full spectrum of his teacher's personality. Blass reportedly asked for him in his final hours.

College & Engagement

During this time, Brad's mother, Catherine, worked at Erickson's Poultry in Bremerton and taught swimming at the YMCA. Jake worked in Seattle as an accountant, but a heart attack in 1955 created difficulties on a number of fronts. Brad curtailed his college studies and worked longer hours at Lent's Mechanical and Plumbing. There were tensions with his brother Gary as well. The brothers fought often. Brad broke his arm during a scuffle that started during an argument about the family's setbacks.

Top: *Harrison Blass from an Olympic College yearbook, late 1960s.*

Bottom: *Brad Kauzlaric, 1955.*

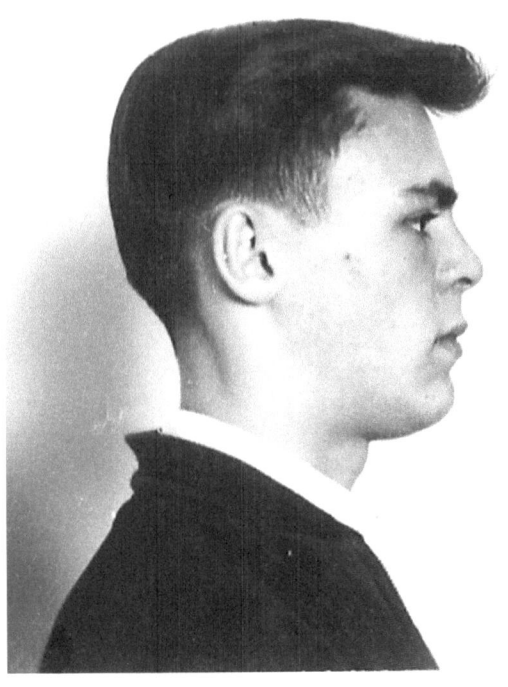

With the challenge of balancing support for his family and finishing his degree, it took longer than expected to complete his studies at Olympic College.

Once he was a full-time student again in 1957, he befriended Korean War veterans Stuart Johnson and Glen Smestad. They would congregate at Graham's Drive-In on Kitsap Way over coffee and cigarettes. For a time, Brad created illustrations for *The Ranger*, the student newspaper, along with his classmate Tom

Biographical Sketch

Stockley. An April Fools' issue in 1956 featuring some off-color humor wasn't received well, and the entire team was dismissed by the college, at least temporarily. Thoroughly chastised, the team returned to college and went back to work on *The Ranger*, though Brad decided to forego the newspaper and instead focus on his classes until he finished his associate degree. Stockley later became the wine columnist for *The Seattle Times* from 1973 to 1989.

During this time, Brad spoke to a young woman named DeAnna Johnson at a college Homecoming Ball in 1956. She was still in high school and was there with a friend of her brother's. Brad had seen her around town but didn't know her name. After their brief meeting he did some sleuthing to remedy that. She wasn't interested in him, it seems, as she stated in an article she wrote for an anniversary edition of the college newspaper forty years later:

Even in the dim light and array of crepe paper streamers and balloons above, I noticed a young man grazing from couple to couple, stopping briefly, and then moving on. He had a shock of dark hair hanging in his face. He looked like a guy from the musical "West Side Story" and out of place despite his pale blue suit. "He's hitting on every girl on the dance floor," my date observed. I agreed, and thought it was terribly crass.

By the time Brad stopped at the couple next to us, I realized he was asking girls to dance. It was the halftime show. There wasn't any dance music at that time, but that didn't stop him. He obviously had a total lack of social protocol. Where was his date? Naturally, I rebuffed him in the haughtiest way possible. Perturbed, yes, but he got my attention.

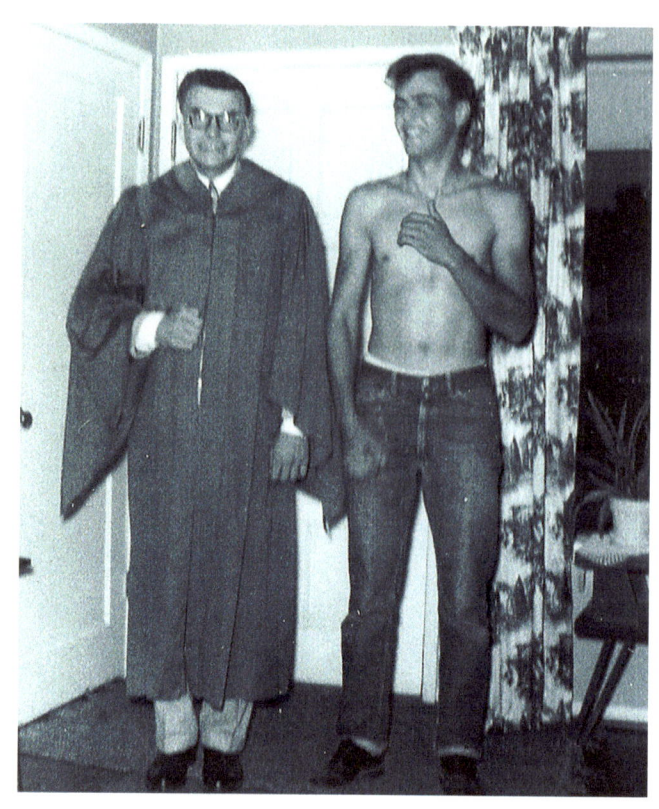

Top, left to right: *Gary and Brad Kauzlaric, 1955.*

Bottom: *Brad's student ID from Olympic College, 1956.*

Biographical Sketch

Assorted art class assignments from Olympic College.

In spite of her initial reaction, Brad's relationship with DeAnna eventually flourished, and the two were engaged in 1958.

Kauzlaric left OC five credits short of graduating to work at ESCO on Harbor Island, a company that supplied sheet metal for the Alaskan oil pipeline project. About the same time, Jake and Catherine bought the Wyatt House on Bainbridge. Brad commuted to work and also helped his father, who was buying and refurbishing old houses on the island for resale. It was here that Kauzlaric established his first real studio space in a large multi-windowed upstairs room that faced an orchard. During this time, he received his first painting commission for an "industrial portrayal" to be hung in ESCO's corporate office in Seattle. He later finished the last credits of his associate's degree in 1962.

Brad quickly made connections in the small but vibrant art community of the island. Brad found some island people; others found him when he became involved with the Bainbridge Arts & Crafts organization, a collective of artists and craftspeople in North Kitsap since 1948. In one of their annual competitions, he entered a mosaic of a rooster. It won an award and was purchased.

Kauzlaric loved the Bainbridge Island of the late 1950s, its collection of characters and laid-back lifestyle. It wasn't unusual for motorists to make way for an elderly couple who habitually drove on the wrong side of the road. Locals recognized the car and simply moved over. Sometimes, after the couple finished shopping, a town policeman would drive them home. On the other side of Puget Sound,

Biographical Sketch

Top: *Rooster template for an early mosaic panel.*

Bottom: *Late 1950s clipping from the* Bremerton Sun.

Kauzlaric would visit delightful antique dealers in the Lynnwood area who served Darjeeling tea, whether a customer was treasure hunting or not. He became acquainted with other young people commuting to work or school in Seattle, and enjoyed pinochle games on the ferry and socializing with them.

Newlywed Life

Brad and DeAnna married in 1958. They moved to a small rental house off Whistle Lake Road in Anacortes, Washington, where Brad had taken a job with Western Disposal. Space was scarce in the couple's first home, so all of the art supplies, props, and still life objects he'd collected were stored in a shed on the property.

One object that Brad kept in the house was "Henrietta," the name Brad gave to the skull of a Native American he found in an abandoned wood stove in a barn on Bainbridge Island. Henrietta was put in a white gift box and carefully wrapped in tissue among wedding gifts stacked in the bedroom. One day, DeAnna opened it, thinking it was a gift to be put away. It was a complete and unappreciated surprise. Brad couldn't understand why she didn't want to share their bedroom with Henrietta. He thought she was very interesting and figured she would be in a painting one day. Many years later, after having some disturbing dreams about Henrietta, Brad made inquiries and repatriated the skull to a local tribe with the assurance that it would be ceremonially re-interred.

Since he wasn't attending college at this time, Brad was eligible for the draft and was soon notified that he was selected for military service. The newlyweds made plans to live apart, with DeAnna remaining in Bremerton. The transitory life of a military wife did not appeal to her. These plans went from theory to practice as Brad reported for his physical and the process began. A stint in the armed forces was not to be, though. A pregnancy test at the last moment came back positive. DeAnna was pregnant with their first son, Keagan. Her physician, also an advisor for the local draft board, made arrangements for a family deferral. Brad's trip to boot camp was averted scarcely a day before he was scheduled to report.

Brad worked with his brother-in-law, Dean Smalley, making frequent trips to other Western Disposal franchises in Renton and Kirkland, Washington. Brad and Dean worked routes throughout the Puget Sound region, getting acquainted with many aspects of Western's operations. Brad eventually moved into a supervisory role, his first experience managing a crew, which included seasoned veterans of garbage collection. This time marked the beginning of an attempt to foster a "tough-guy" image because he thought, at age 22, it would be necessary to get the job done. Though friendly and outgoing with close friends, a gruff, abrupt demeanor was often what new acquaintances encountered when meeting Brad for the first time.

Brad and DeAnna's first year was quite busy socially. Their one bedroom rental home hosted a steady stream of family and friends in all but one weekend during the summer of 1958. The mattress came off their bed

Top: *Brad & DeAnna Kauzlaric's engagement photo, 1958.*

Bottom: *Brad & DeAnna Kauzlaric's wedding, 1958.*

so they could sleep on the front room floor and offer a place to sleep for guests. It was September before they realized their quaint sofa was also a foldout bed.

While living in Anacortes, Brad was a member of the Lion's Club. The Lion's had a unique way of encouraging regular attendance. If a member missed a meeting without a good excuse, the club left a rooster on their doorstep. Besides being awakened by the early crowing, it had to be fed and watered for a week until the next meeting. It's probably a coincidence, but a crowing rooster figure appears several times in Brad's early mosaics.

Brad and DeAnna didn't stay long in Anacortes. They moved the following year to Renton, a city at the south end of Lake Washington, once again following work for Western Disposal. Their first son, Keagan, was born during the year they lived there, in 1959. Boeing, located in the area, was growing rapidly during the late 1950s, so it was difficult to find a suitable house for the young family. The couple lived briefly in a two-bedroom duplex, where Brad converted one bedroom into an art studio. After having kept his art materials in a shed, this was a great improvement, even though the exorbitant use of the family's limited space scandalized his mother-in-law. The Kauzlarics finally settled in a more spacious three-bedroom house in the Maplewood neighborhood.

Though living in Renton, a city just south of Seattle, Brad's garbage routes for Western Disposal took him to a number of communities around Kirkland, a town just across Lake Washington from Seattle. Kirkland is now easily reached from Seattle via one of two floating bridges that cross Lake Washington,

Brad, DeAnna, and their first son, Keagan, in East Bremerton, 1963.

but that was still years away. At the time, a trip from Seattle to Kirkland still involved taking a ferry across Lake Washington. Years later, Brad often recalled the colorful characters and merchants he met along Lake Washington Boulevard in the town situated on the lakefront.

Despite his demanding work schedule, he attempted to devote time to developing and selling his works. Brad sold a number of paintings and produced commissioned works for both collectors and corporate clients.

Distant Worlds

In a rare break from his usual pace that year, Brad took some time off during a particularly bad spell of wet, winter weather and spent part of each day laying on the living room rug in front of a roaring fireplace reading a book from the stack nearby. Kauzlaric loved science fiction and would usually consume an entire novel in one sitting. Time and space concerned him because they were both in short supply between the demands of a physically taxing job and his growing family at home. Like the protagonist of a science fiction novel, he may have thought time and space didn't truly exist, as well. In his world of ideas and idealism, he began to develop themes related to the constraints of time and space. The interplay of space in many of Brad's oil paintings, such as *September 34th* (1995, p. 86), speak to his strong feelings about space, whether the clash of nature and man in outer space or the struggles of a person's inner space. Time appears in his work repeatedly, both in the form of

Outside the home of Kauzlaric's in-laws, George and Ferne Johnson, in East Bremerton, 1963.

Biographical Sketch

clocks and timepieces but also in the form of passing, temporal phenomena seen in nature or, for instance, an old barn slowly collapsing on itself. Brad thought these were worthwhile themes, which he explored for many years to come.

Brad also loved open spaces and chafed at his sense of being confined in any living situation where neighbors could be seen and heard. This may have had some connection to his job driving a garbage truck. Being surrounded by the trash of his fellow humans, traffic and noisy machinery all day at work, and then a busy household at home made peace and tranquility a rare commodity. Brad began serious examination of Alaska as a place to live. His wife did not embrace the idea with much enthusiasm. Still, he read everything he could about the newly minted state and sought the advice of Elsie and Wayne Bailey, neighbors who once lived there. As a pilot, Wayne had firsthand information, and much of it was positive. This fueled Brad's interest in "natural independence" and many years of subscriptions to *Alaska Magazine*, which he always read cover to cover. On his second trip to Alaska, in the early 1970s, DeAnna went with him and they explored the area around Haines, a city in Southeast Alaska, where electricity from the town's noisy generator was dependent on regular deliveries of oil. Brad and DeAnna realized that life up north wasn't perfect and came with its own set of challenges. On their ferry ride back to Juneau, the appeal faded with the twilight when they reconciled their fact-findings with the logistics of relocating. His trips to Alaska would have some impact on Brad creatively, though, as it deepened his appreciation of

Biographical Sketch

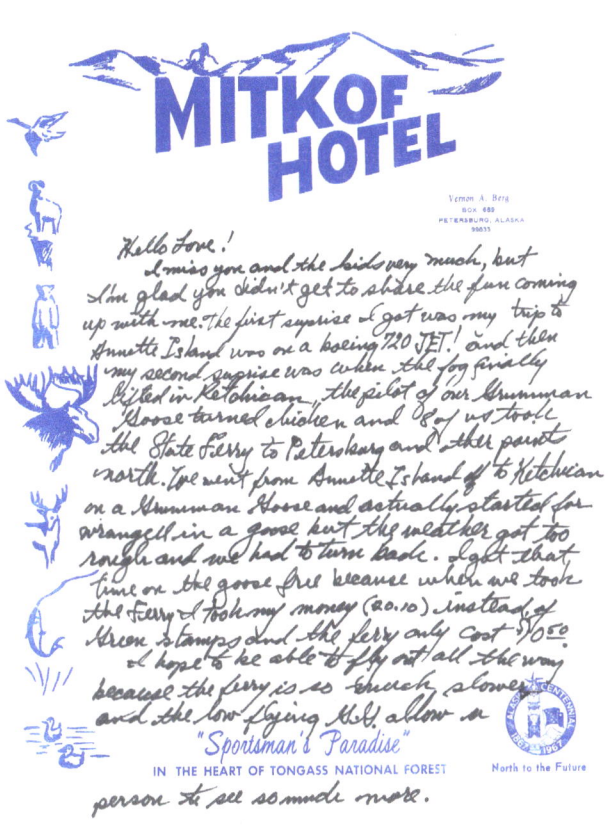

indigenous Haida and Tlingit artwork. This emerged in commissioned work for P. R. Hart & Company in 1970 and his wood carving *Shaman's Eye* (1975, p. 185).

Back In Kitsap

Brad's time with Western Disposal lead to a job with Bremerton-based Brem-Air Disposal, which brought him and his family back to Kitsap County in 1960. Western Washington was entering a vibrant, exciting time. The upcoming Century 21 World's Fair in Seattle was in the works as Seattle worked diligently to bolster its image, both as a city and as a cultural hub for the Northwest. It was a time when Seattle artists were garnering national attention. One of the World's Fair building designers, Minoru Yamasaki, would go on to design the World Trade Center in New York. Noted painter and mosaic artist Paul Horiuchi created a large, striking mosaic for the fairgrounds. Several fountains by George Tsutakawa graced sidewalks and squares of Seattle. These Seattleites of Japanese descent had a decided influence on Brad. This manifested most clearly in his tree paintings from 1978 to 1989 (pp. 104–115). It also drove a preference for what Brad called the "simple design, but elaborate execution" seen in many of his still life works.

Across Puget Sound in Kitsap County, Brad's life was filled with the everyday work of establishing a new home. Brad and DeAnna tackled the remodeling of a house on North Perry Avenue on Bremerton's east side. They initially rented the house from DeAnna's brother Monty at no cost, with the condition that they make substantial improvements to the house.

Opposite: *Dolphin mosaic from Ocean Shores, 1965.*

Above: *A letter to DeAnna from Alaska, 1968.*

Below: *Kauzlaric in Alaska, 1973.*

Biographical Sketch

Brad and DeAnna soon purchased the house as they continued the renovations. Brad's brother-in-law replaced the foundation, furnace, and roof as part of the arrangement. "I thought about using it for a horse barn," Monty said of the state of the house, "but I was afraid the horse would fall through the floor." Brad and Monty replaced most of the windows and put sheetrock in the kitchen.

Brad's father was impressed with the way the remodeled kitchen turned out. "I didn't know you knew how to build cabinets or lay Formica," he said at the time, implying these skills could have been used when they were working together on Bainbridge Island. Brad's reply was, "You never asked." The studio space was in the basement, with a convenient trap door to the kitchen that DeAnna would use to call Brad up to dinner.

Brad produced a number of substantial mosaic works during this time, including a large pair of seahorses for the wall of a hotel ballroom in Ocean Shores (pp. 208–209), Washington. Other works included a wall mosaic of buffalo (p. 129). Brad and DeAnna didn't own a good quality camera, so only murky Polaroid photos exist of these works today.

A second son, Kenton, was born in 1961, but he died two days later due to complications of a premature

Top: *The Kauzlaric family, 1965.*

Middle, left to right: *Klinton, Brad, Keagan, Clayton, DeAnna, and Alicia Kauzlaric, 1967.*

Bottom: *At the beach near Brownsville, 1968.*

birth. Daughter Alicia was adopted in 1963. Another son, Clayton, was born in 1964. He initially suffered the same health issues as Kenton, so DeAnna couldn't bring herself to visit him in neonatal care at the hospital in Bremerton. Brad had more courage and regularly visited, still wearing his garbage man's uniform and work boots. The nursery supervisor would meet Brad at the door with scrubs after he had sanitized his hands and face so he could visit the struggling newborn. Whether it was this extra attention or a peculiarity of his condition was not known, but Clayton survived. Brad and DeAnna had another son, Klinton, late in 1965.

Now supporting a family of six, Brad worked to balance his goals as an artist with family responsibilities. With the arrival of the youngest Kauzlaric children, the family needed more room yet again. He and DeAnna worked to finish a new house in the Gilberton community near Brownsville, Washington, in 1965. Prior to their first house in Bremerton, Kauzlaric often lacked a studio space of any real size. The Gilberton house had an unfinished basement, most of which he would be dedicated to a more ideal workspace. Here, he continued to produce occasional commissioned works and personal projects for shows and exhibits in Kitsap County. His projects included portraits, still lifes, placemat designs for a restaurant supplier, and several more mosaic projects. Among these was his most ambitious mosaic series, a

The Kauzlaric home in Gilberton, near Brownsville, Washington, 1969.

complete *Stations of the Cross* (pp. 151–164) for Holy Trinity Catholic church in Bremerton. Despite the challenges, this was a highly productive time of his career in terms of artistic output. His studio was directly below the family's bedrooms, so the strains of his radio could be heard upstairs as he painted late into the night. While painting, he preferred listening to classical or jazz music, but he had a fondness for bluegrass and polka as well.

This was also an active era for Brad's interest in politics, which were decidedly conservative for many years. During the 1960s, it was common for artists to be politically active, though few volunteered for the presidential campaign of Arizona senator Barry Goldwater. The neighborhood postal carrier, Walt Nutter, noticed Brad's interests and engaged in lively political discussions with him. The two became fast friends. Walt became a regular in the Kauzlaric household

Kitsap Sun, Bremerton, Wash., used by permission.

Brad's portrait of State Representative Arnold Wang, presented in 1967.

Biographical Sketch

Kauzlaric showing pieces at a local bank, 1970.

throughout the year. Visits often centered around a game of chess or cribbage. When the family went on swimming trips near the Brownsville marina, Walt was usually in the water when the family arrived, floating in a leisurely manner far from the shore. He was at every Christmas dinner and major holiday outing for years to come.

Biographical Sketch

Above: *Kauzlaric's parents, Jake and Kay, at Seabeck, 1949.*

Below: *Notice announcing a contest win for a still life painting, 1973.*

Kitsap Sun, Bremerton, Wash., used by permission.

Only a Day Job

Brad initially took the job with Western Disposal in 1958 strictly for the income. He saw no future in sanitation work, except as a way to earn a living. Decades later, at Brem-Air Disposal, he still saw his job as a temporary thing. In darker moods, he groused about missed opportunities that his job and responsibilities required of him. Despite this, he made a significant contribution to the regional sanitation industry. He helped to organize a public relations program on recycling and promoted its mascot, "Perry the Penguin." His intimate knowledge of Kitsap County roads brought increased efficiency to the routes he designed and managed over the years. He wrote a brief history of commercial garbage hauling and disposal in the early 1990s and assisted in positioning Brem-Air Disposal on the forefront of bio-friendly methods of operation and the recycling. The disposal crews either hated or loved Kauzlaric—most likely the former as he was a strict taskmaster. He was a loyal Teamster for several decades and reluctantly left the union while in management. Brad's gruff demeanor while on the job at Brem-Air was different from the easy-going persona he adopted with friends, but he thought it necessary to maintain discipline and the standard of work he expected.

Judgment

One day in Seattle, Kauzlaric happened to share a taxi with one of the jurors of a Seattle art show he had seen. Not wanting to miss the opportunity, Brad questioned the judgment of a juror who happened to be an art professor at the University of Washington.

Drafting table at Brad's Seabeck mosaic studio.

Tossing a barb or two, the juror asked how the opinion of a garbage man could be relevant. Brad countered with, "I can safely say I know garbage when I see it."

Brad retained a lifelong ambivalence about art competitions that were judged by juries or panels of experts. He was perfectly fine with a public vote, but he disliked putting his work up for judgment by a select few. At least in part as a result, he often avoided opportunities to display his work, sometimes feeling that the world would discover him sooner or later based on the merits of his work.

Brad's work was shown in a few Northwest galleries during the 1970's and 80's, including Sandy Bradley Gallery in Seattle's Fremont district and the Carolyn Hartness Gallery in Pioneer Square, but despite his steady output of paintings and mosaics one-man gallery exhibitions were relatively rare. Most pieces he sold were to family, friends and coworkers. Commissioned works did occur from time to time, but securing them required more time and salesmanship than Brad could realistically muster. Contests and competitions also lacked appeal for him. What shows he did have were usually small collections of his works exhibited in the lobbies of local banks and businesses.

Brad forged ahead. His output of mosaics increased as his style became more detailed and distinctive. He

Biographical Sketch

also ventured into making "cement windows," stained glass with frames build of rebar-reinforced cement. An ingenious frame/form system he derived from his mosaic construction made curved, graceful frames possible, in spite of the heavy material they used. His largest window was built for his friends Bill and Laura King's new house in east Bremerton (p. 180). A later owner of the house liked the window well enough to take it with them when they sold the house. Another mosaic project included holy water fonts for Our Lady Star of the Sea parish in Bremerton (p. 165).

Seabeck

The house in Brownsville soon proved too confining, both for the family as the four Kauzlaric children grew, and for the scope of Brad's work. More space became a priority by the late 1960s. He and DeAnna started the process of looking for a place where they could accommodate both needs.

Brad and DeAnna envisioned a home they could design and build from the ground up, with room for a separate mosaic studio. They visited properties for a number of years, mostly in Kitsap County, sometimes venturing across Hood Canal with the four Kauzlaric children in the back seat of their '68 Buick Wildcat.

Brad had an affinity for the Seabeck area of Kitsap County since first visiting with his parents in the late 1940s. He and DeAnna eventually bought acreage in the Lone Rock area of Seabeck, near the end of Pioneer Road, in 1975. Brad paid earnest money on ten acres that was later divided into two parcels, one

Kitsap Sun, Bremerton, Wash., used by permission.

Above: *Clippings from exhibits around Kitsap County, late 1970s.*

Below: *Kauzlaric kids and Brad working on the new Seabeck house,*

of which was sold. They later purchased another five acres along the family's lengthy access road in the early 1980s. It didn't take many trips to the property before DeAnna and Brad wanted to speed up their building schedule and live there full time.

The couple set about building their dream home. They designed the house themselves, while implementation of their vision was carried out by a creative local building contractor named Wally Carlson. The Kauzlarics defrayed the cost of construction by pitching in, and even the kids spent many hours hauling lumber and swinging hammers.

The family lived in a mobile home for a year and a half while the property and house took shape, living the first weeks without electricity or running water. It was a big change for the family as a whole, moving from the relatively close environs of Gilberton to the less-developed Seabeck property. Brad designed a separate studio for painting in the house and a space devoted to mosaic and sculpture construction in a

Above: *The Kauzlaric house at Seabeck, 2007.*

Below: *Kauzlaric in 1984.*

Biographical Sketch

barn-shaped outbuilding. The barn space allowed for easier construction of larger mosaics, plus storage of more material, props, and random objects he found on his garbage route.

The painting studio featured a large, wall-mounted easel that Brad designed and constructed himself. This allowed him to work on larger paintings than he had previously done in Brownsville and in earlier workspaces. He sometimes said the purpose of his artwork was to enable a viewer to see the world the way he did, and these larger, more expansive works were a way to do that more effectively.

This period also saw a transition from the Masonite he used for nearly all his prior paintings to more traditional canvas, now that he had enough room to stretch and prep large canvasses properly. He had worked almost exclusively on Masonite for nearly two decades, valuing the dense, pressed wood composite as an affordable, stable surface that could be cut easily without the added time and effort required to prep a conventional canvas. But it was heavy when used in larger panels, so a switch to canvas, which was much lighter, was a logical choice.

The larger paintings he produced at the Seabeck house represent some of his most detailed and involved creations. Brad still turned out smaller works on his more typical painting easel, while the larger paintings sometimes took years to complete. This was in part due to his preference for working with small brushstrokes using fine sable brushes and his obsession with even the most minor details. Brad was fond of laying down very detailed underpaintings, which themselves

Biographical Sketch

would have stood up as finished works, only to build additional thin layers on top, a glaze technique called scumbling. This was a way of achieving the illusion of transparency or the glowing effect of light shining through cloth.

The dynamics of the Kauzlaric household were starting to change, too. DeAnna joined the workforce with a part-time job as a communications specialist at Olympic College in 1978. This created some tension, given Kauzlaric's traditional attitude and sense of pride as the family's sole breadwinner. Their eldest son, Keagan, graduated from high school the previous year and was soon out on his own. With Alicia, Clayton, and Klinton still in the house, college expenses ahead, and the ongoing effort to finish their new home, it was a logical step. Her work at the college was also something DeAnna enjoyed. There were more changes ahead by the late 1980s. The remaining Kauzlaric children grew up and moved out. DeAnna's role at OC became a full time position. Brad and DeAnna found themselves in an empty nest with options and choices they didn't have previously. It was finally feasible for Brad to pursue art full-time. But he didn't make this choice immediately. Then, in 1991, Brad was injured while operating a top-loading dumpster truck in Silverdale. This was the trigger that made his departure from the workforce an easy decision in 1992. He was then 55 years old.

Left: *At work on* Alder Lace, *1988.*

Below Left: *Brad in 1986.*

The float outside Brad's studio window was incorporated into several of his surrealistic paintings, including September 34th *and the* Channel Marker *series.*

Biographical Sketch

Looking Back on the Route

Brad's career in sanitation may have begun as an expedient way to earn money while he looked to the day when he could do art exclusively, but it lasted for 33 years. Like any major chapter of someone's life, he forged friendships and relationships that went beyond the daily details of the job itself. Brad could be famously combative and cantankerous, but a number of people in the garbage business eased difficult days with their sense of humor and generosity of spirit. Shop foreman Harold Adkisson and his wife Virginia were among these people. Brad seldom saw eye-to-eye with Brem-Air owner Don Lindgren, but he and his wife Beverly were among the most prominent buyers of Brad's artwork.

It would be easy to view those decades as a story about doing a job to support a family of six while he dreamed of artistic success. He typically avoided advancement and deeper involvement in his profession. Be on time, do a good job, and go home was his overriding philosophy. It was a "day job," but the impact of Brad's sanitation job on his art was immense.

There were material advantages to driving a garbage truck. Brad trained landfill workers to be on the lookout for useful materials he needed for mosaics, including specimens of Carrara plate and colored glass. Far from being "junk," these items were of high quality but were nevertheless often thrown away by building contractors and homeowners. He set aside used car batteries and scrap metal to trade for these discarded goods. Broken bottles and crockery from the family dinner table sometimes found their way into mosaics. Breaking a dish was never viewed as a bad thing in the Kauzlaric household.

Kauzlaric's still lifes and surrealistic paintings often portray items he found in the trash and brought home to his studio. The years he worked a garbage route were mostly before American society became conscious of collectibles and the value of old objects.

Kauzlaric in his painting studio from a profile story in the Kitsap Sun, *1990.*

Kitsap Sun, Bremerton, Wash., used by permission.

MacKenzie

In 1979 Brad painted *Lion's Rampant*, a portrait of Bruce MacKenzie. Brad and Bruce met through the friendship of their sons Klinton and Rob, who attended Seabeck Elementary together. With his Scot-Norwegian old-world charm, knack for storytelling, and sharp wit, Bruce cultivated friendships easily. His long-time love of wooden boats and water were natural outgrowths of his background as a ship's captain, sea adventurer, and, later in his life, shipping manager and consultant for the Port of Tacoma. He and Kauzlaric hit it off immediately when they met in 1977 and were friends the rest of their lives.

There was no discussion about what Bruce might wear for his portrait, so he came to his first sitting wearing a red and white shirt imprinted with the Lion Rampant, the Scottish Royal Banner of Arms. Each rampant was approximately one inch high. Bruce was convinced that Kauzlaric would either ignore the shirt design entirely or ask MacKenzie to wear something else. Instead, Kauzlaric saw it as a challenge and painted every one of the little lions. To aid in this effort, he drew a scale pattern to use as a reference when he worked on the painting after MacKenzie's sittings. To Bruce's chagrin, the sessions didn't take as much time as he expected. The portrait itself is, sadly, among the missing pieces documented in the *Missing Works* chapter (p. 204).

Biographical Sketch

His collection of props included a pilot's headgear from World War II, vintage clocks, watches, broken musical instruments, hunting decoys, vintage fishing reels, a ship's reflector from the age of sail, obscure scientific instruments, music boxes, vintage ice skates, and countless other objects. His studio was filled with bins and boxes that barely contained the overflow of ephemera that caught his eye. His studio was generally off limits to his children, but its endless supply of curios made it irresistible.

Another aspect of the job that made it an invaluable source of ideas was the nature of the work itself. His route took him through city streets and some of Kitsap County's remote rural byways. He took note of what he saw, from quiet moments of striking natural beauty to random interactions with the people he met. These sometimes sparked ideas and stories that were later translated into portraits, surreal vistas, and visual metaphors. Brad often said that he enjoyed watching Kitsap County wake up.

A theme that appears repeatedly in Kauzlaric's art was change, which went hand-in-hand with time and permanence. His years working his sanitation routes on the streets of a rapidly growing county gave Kauzlaric a firsthand view of its shifting landscape. This can be seen in sketches and paintings of the barns and pastures of Silverdale and central Kitsap

Above: *Kauzlaric doing chores on the Seabeck property, 2004.*

Opposite: *Some of the objects and props kept in Kauzlaric's mosaic studio.*

County. His still life and surrealistic paintings usually feature once-discarded items shown in a new context as something beautiful and interesting. Vanishing, overlooked places and ephemera found their way into many of his works.

He preferred to go through a work day without a partner, or swamper, who rode along to help the driver. This was before the days of automated lifts that raise and empty garbage cans, so it was more work for a lone driver. Yet Kauzlaric had a stated preference for this, perhaps so he could be alone with his thoughts and ideas. He could also be particular about procedures and the details of the job. In spite of this, some coworkers who worked by his side became close friends, most notably Bill King, who not only visited the Kauzlaric household many times but also participated in the creation of one of Brad's painting when he posed for *The Fishing Hole* (1974, p. 82). King and his wife Laura would later amass the largest collections of Brad's work outside his own.

Before he left Brem-Air Disposal, Brad started teaching art students from his Seabeck home. Over the course of several years, about a dozen pupils came out to the Kauzlaric home for lessons about once a week. He expanded his teaching efforts, offering evening painting classes at Olympic College, where his own artistic ambitions began. Brad taught at OC between 1986 and 1988, though he only offered classes for a few quarters.

Biographical Sketch

Another development that had a large impact on his work was an increased number of trips to Seattle at around this time. Brad's wife, DeAnna, decided to finish her bachelor's degree starting in 1989. This took her to evening classes at the University of Washington. Brad accompanied her and explored areas near Seattle's University District while she attended her classes. Sometimes he passed the time at the charming coffee shop situated in the Burke Museum. Kauzlaric also ambled around Fremont, where he met artists and craftspeople, particularly at the then-vibrant Fremont Foundry. Kauzlaric soon formed new associations and friendships. He talked excitedly about meeting and talking with other artists, which was a new experience for him.

Kauzlaric also took this time to meet gallery owners and show his portfolio. This change in surroundings and his efforts to promote himself led to the largest showing of his works in his lifetime, at the Lawson Gallery in 1993. This was also the largest retrospective of his works, though once again the few pieces sold at the show were mostly to friends and acquaintances.

Once DeAnna finished her degree, Brad's visits to Seattle dropped off as he retreated to his Seabeck studio, where he was always most comfortable.

Above: *Kauzlaric teaching at Olympic College, 1989.*

Opposite: *Kauzlaric at his retrospective show at the Lawson Gallery, 1993.*

Off the Truck

After retiring from sanitation work in 1992, Brad cast about for new projects and pursuits. The time he previously lacked was suddenly abundant. Projects continued on the couple's sprawling property at Seabeck. Like many home construction projects, the basement and other parts of the house took decades to complete. Brad added many creative touches to the house, including three of his distinctive cement windows in the entryway and festive floral mosaics for the sill dividing the kitchen and dining areas.

Brad continued to design and construct mosaics and sculptures with hopes of placing them in appropriate locations. This included a life-sized mosaic of Mary, *Stella Maris* (p. 166), and a mock-up of a statue.

It's difficult to say whether this was a time of great progress for Kauzlaric as an artist. It seems that his decades of steady production declined as the need to escape into art became less urgent. It's possible that without the continuous input his sanitation job provided, his creative output diminished as well. His painting and mosaic work continued steadily, but his yearly output never really increased. The time he once had so little of was now abundant, but he was just as likely to spend time working on odds and ends around the Seabeck property, gardening, cutting firewood, and almost daily visits to Seabeck Landing.

The Lawson Gallery show, 1993.

One contributing factor that may have taken a toll on his productivity and creative energies was Kauzlaric's use of alcohol. At his father's funeral reception he was chided for not drinking, but as he got older, he became more dependent on its effects. What started as a couple beers after work at times became a problem, which led to an incident in which he drove his Volkswagen bug into a tree. His already varied mood swings grew more pronounced when he drank, leading to occasional outbursts and conflicts at family and social gatherings. It's difficult to assess what impact this ultimately had on his success as an artist. In spite of years of steady drinking, Kauzlaric had a knack for keeping his life compartmentalized. Still, after decades of this pattern, it must have had some effect on his artistic endeavors.

The Gallery

DeAnna suggested a new approach for his art career: opening an art gallery. The post office in Seabeck was moved in 1997 to new quarters on the Seabeck-Holly Road, and DeAnna proposed that they lease the old post office space on the waterfront and convert it into an art gallery. They opened the Seabeck Art Gallery a few months later. The gallery was a venue for Brad's artwork as well as a cooperative for about twenty local artists.

The gallery displayed the work of Ken Lundemo, Ann Quinn, John Hoover, Mary Lou Slaughter, Pam and Andrew Buck, and others. Lundemo was a founder of the Collective Visions gallery in Bremerton. He created distinctive raku-glazed pottery and was a friend during Brad's college days. The two were only distantly acquainted during the intervening decades, but they rekindled their friendship through the Seabeck Gallery. Brad had long admired the work of John Hoover, a wood carver of Aleut-Russian descent. He sought him out through other Mason County artists. The two artists hit it off almost immediately and became fast friends. Ann Quinn and her husband had known the Kauzlarics for years, but her photography and paintings were a revelation. Brad felt compelled to show her work as well. He carefully chose those he considered to be among the best potters, carvers, photographers, jewelry makers, and similar fields. He took delight in representing the talent and dedication of other artists, and he found a new appreciation for the art world by working closely with these individuals.

Brad was particularly fond of John Hoover. For years after the storefront gallery was closed, the sight of a raven would prompt Brad to call his Aleut woodcarver friend. They shared some things in common, such as the tough physical labor of their early "day job" years. John was a commercial fisherman with a wry sense of humor. Brad later painted his portrait, which was made more fun by John insisting that he was the better painter.

Seabeck attracts visitors from around the Pacific Northwest, the US, and the world with its natural beauty. The gallery's guest book held the signatures of visitors from all over the globe. The marina was busy, but business at the gallery was usually slow. Brad used some of this time to dream up new projects, and write bits of poetry and doggerel. This included text and illustrations for an unpublished children's book called "The Billygoo Bird."

The Seabeck Art Gallery opening, 1998.

Biographical Sketch

As usual, what he saw in his surroundings found its way into a series of paintings. He began the *Channel Marker* series (1996–1997, pp. 87, 102, 103) based on the sights and sounds of the small, bustling marina. When one of the paintings was in the gallery, a visitor asked where the location of it might be. Having a bit of fun with the question, Brad proceeded to direct the fellow to the Hansville area of North Kitsap, all the while taking in the inquirer's earnest attempt to jot down the directions on a notepad. Thinking he had gone far enough, they both laughed when Brad explained the real "site" was in his head.

Brad enjoyed his time as a gallery owner. He and DeAnna even considered purchasing the building and converting the upstairs apartment into a permanent residence for a time, but cost and logistics made this too impractical. Brad also took issue with local leaders over issues of parking and water access in the cluster of buildings that constituted Seabeck's small but active marina. He was asked years later to become involved in other civic issues, but he had to decline. Kauzlaric was running out of energy, and the gallery was taking time away from time in his shop and studio. He decided he wasn't cut of real proprietor's cloth, so he closed the storefront two years later. He kept the Seabeck Art Gallery name on his business license and moved the telephone line to his mosaic shop on his property.

After closing the gallery, Brad's life settled into a quieter home-based routine. He kept busy with projects around the property, including finishing touches on the house and a major kitchen remodel. He continued to stoke the little wood stove in his mosaic shop, where he listened to the radio and worked on both mosaics and sculptures. Regular swims at the Bremerton Tennis & Athletic Club were often a time of reflection, even prayer, as Kauzlaric contemplated future projects and mulled over ideas.

The Halibut

One of Brad's most distinctive later mosaics was of a large halibut (1999, p. 144) commissioned by Suzanne Arness from Kingston. Flounders—juvenile halibut found in many of Washington's coastal waters—had long fascinated Brad for their changing nature. In a rare moment in which he talked about his own history and the inspiration for a piece of artwork, he wrote a description for Arness.

Opposite top: *Works on display at the Seabeck Art Gallery, 1998.*

Opposite bottom: *At work on an unfinished* Channel Marker *painting, 2004.*

Right: *With a design for a marine life mosaic, 2004.*

Biographical Sketch

Top: *At work on* Holy Flounder, *2000.*
Bottom: *Tools for Kauzlaric's mosaic work.*

Biographical Sketch

HALIBUT (holy flounder) in Harding Creek 1950

There they were. Fat flounders. And, we ran barefoot in the mud and tide chasing them with our barely sharpened alders. The Starry Flounders were fat and sassy. Maybe it was all the Watland chicken manure dumped into the Creek in those days. The fish were too wormy to eat but fast to the chase and skewer.

The Aske boys (Roald and Lawrence) showed my brother Gary and I how to spear them in what is now known as Dogfish Creek. This is the same place we skinny-dipped in frigid waters. As grandsons of Brevig, the chicken hatchery operator who lived off Finn Hill Road, the Aske boys were a boyhood source of local information and adventure in Poulsbo.

My fascination with this particular flounder centers on their in-between stage, knowing that, unlike other flat fish, they can decide to be either right- or left-eyed in their permanent residency. Their motion as they coast so close to the bottom requires a total Puget Sound relationship: thus, the background of all native materials in the Halibut panel.

All designs happen as the instinct and drawings merge, but for me the image is always in my "mind's eye" before it is built. My decision to use this Halibut influenced the size of the work. Custom-cut mosaic makes a bold statement. The strength of this design is as natural as my youthful discoveries: predatory and as unpredictable.

Depending on how you look at it… this is THE fish that got away.

Brad Kauzlaric 4/2000

The mosaic is a striking creation of black glass set in native materials plucked from local beaches.

Cultivating a Look

Over the years, Kauzlaric carefully cultured his appearance and demeanor as one of a cantankerous codger. When extensive dental work and oral surgeries called for a new tooth, he always opted for gold instead of porcelain or materials that would look natural. He enjoyed flashing a gold-toothed grin, even in his thirties.

Biographical Sketch

As a young man, Brad said he couldn't wait to get gray hair, though he never mentioned being anxious to lose his hair. His head was mostly bald by the time he was in his sixties. He still spent a great deal of time outdoors, so he built up a collection of distinctive hats. His wardrobe included Irish walking hats, painter hats, and the ever-present beret. He bought the berets at Byrnie Utz Hats on Union Street in Seattle and preferred those made in Greece. This, along with his gray hair tied back in a short ponytail and Birkenstock sandals, gave Brad a distinctly artistic appearance, though ironically one he might have railed against in his younger days.

The Closing Chapter

But Brad had reached the point in his life where the affectations of age came without extra encouragement. His sense of how fleeting time was must have grown more acute with the passing of his younger brother Gary, in 1999, and his mother Catherine, in 2001.

He continued to produce works, creating a few commissions and portraits, but several larger paintings sat unfinished on his easels. He toyed with ideas for a mosaic series based on the faces of former colleagues and coworkers rendered as clowns. Kauzlaric also continued to lay out drawings for ambitious marine mosaics, all of which were left in stacks in his studio.

His family continued on their way in life as well. The Kauzlaric children all married and had kids of their own. Brad and DeAnna saw the addition of eight grandchildren: Stephanie, Ashley, Derek, Arianna, Kaija, Kateri, Oliver, and Kian.

This didn't mean life was always tranquil. Brad counted many neighbors among his closest friends, but he was defensive and protective when it came to issues of property and his personal space. As adjacent acreage was slowly developed and occupied, Brad was sometimes embroiled in minor spats over access roads and noise issues.

Ironically, Brad's own habit of shooting his guns for fun and target practice raised the ire of some homeowners in the new housing subdivision located just through the trees behind Brad and DeAnna's home. This, combined with Brad's impulsive nature, lead to the accidental demise of one family pet and the inexplicable shooting of a neighbor's peacock after it wandered onto the Kauzlaric property. The local sheriff's deputies were contacted, resulting in a settlement with the neighbors.

As he approached the age of 70, Brad was still cantankerous, but he was slowing down. Discomfort from a hip had bothered him for several years, making some of his favorite pastimes like rowing and stomping through the local forests more difficult. After years of nagging by friends and family, he finally sought replacement surgery in the fall of 2006. For a time, it appeared that with his recuperation he would be able to resume his old habits.

Kauzlaric would see his seventy-first birthday, but only just. Increasing fatigue, weight loss, and vague discomfort was at first thought to be an after-effect of the hip surgery, but the situation was more serious. In 2007, the time he contemplated, portrayed, and carefully measured ran out. In March, DeAnna called their children to tell them that Brad Kauzlaric had been diagnosed with terminal colon cancer. The cancer had already spread, and there was no viable course of treatment he was willing to consider. Brad had always been adamant about his quality of life and was firmly against being sustained by machinery or medication. He opted to undergo surgery with the goal of bypassing an intestinal blockage. There was hope that this would give Brad another three to six months of life at his beloved home in Seabeck, but that was not to be. The surgery was difficult, and the surgeons were unable to complete the procedure in one session. Brad was kept in a medically induced coma, awaiting another surgery, but his vital signs were already fading. DeAnna summoned their children again, just ten days after the initial diagnosis. Brad Kauzlaric died at Harrison Memorial Hospital in Bremerton on April 2, 2007, surrounded by his family.

As with any creative individual, Kauzlaric left behind many unfinished works, from partially finished canvases to rough ideas hastily scrawled on scraps of paper. Within a year of his death, some effort was made to document the considerable collection of Kauzlaric's work at the Seabeck house, which also included countless sketches, designs, models, and notes. This process soon moved beyond the artwork still in the possession of the Kauzlaric family to include paintings and mosaics Kauzlaric had sold (or given away) throughout his career. This volume is the result of that effort. Though by no means complete, it conveys the scope, quality, and variety of Brad Kauzlaric's artwork. He always preferred to let art speak for itself, but his artwork also speaks volumes about him—far more than mere words could convey.

Early Works

Above: *A palette used by Kauzlaric as an art student on the back of a piece of art board, 1957.*

No one still living knows to what extent Brad Kauzlaric exhibited artistic skill or inclination before college. Nothing indicates that he was a child prodigy or artistically inclined while young. The picture we have of him is of an inquisitive, active young man who loved the outdoors. He always possessed a keen mind and was able to read by the age of three.

The student work only hints at the artist he would become. These are mostly standard assignments from his basic training in common media, including sketches, oil paints, pastels, still lifes, and life drawing. From the hundreds of assignments that were found piled in corners of his studio and shop, a handful were chosen for inclusion here.

After graduating from Olympic College, Kauzlaric's work underwent a number of noticeable changes. We only have a few works done between then and his first truly dedicated studio space in Brownsville, Washington, but the leap in polish, style, and self-assurance between the early 1960s to the 1970s is striking. His paintings became less impressionistic, favoring a more crisp, almost photographic level of detail in later works.

Early Works

Oil painting exercises, 1957.

55

Early Works

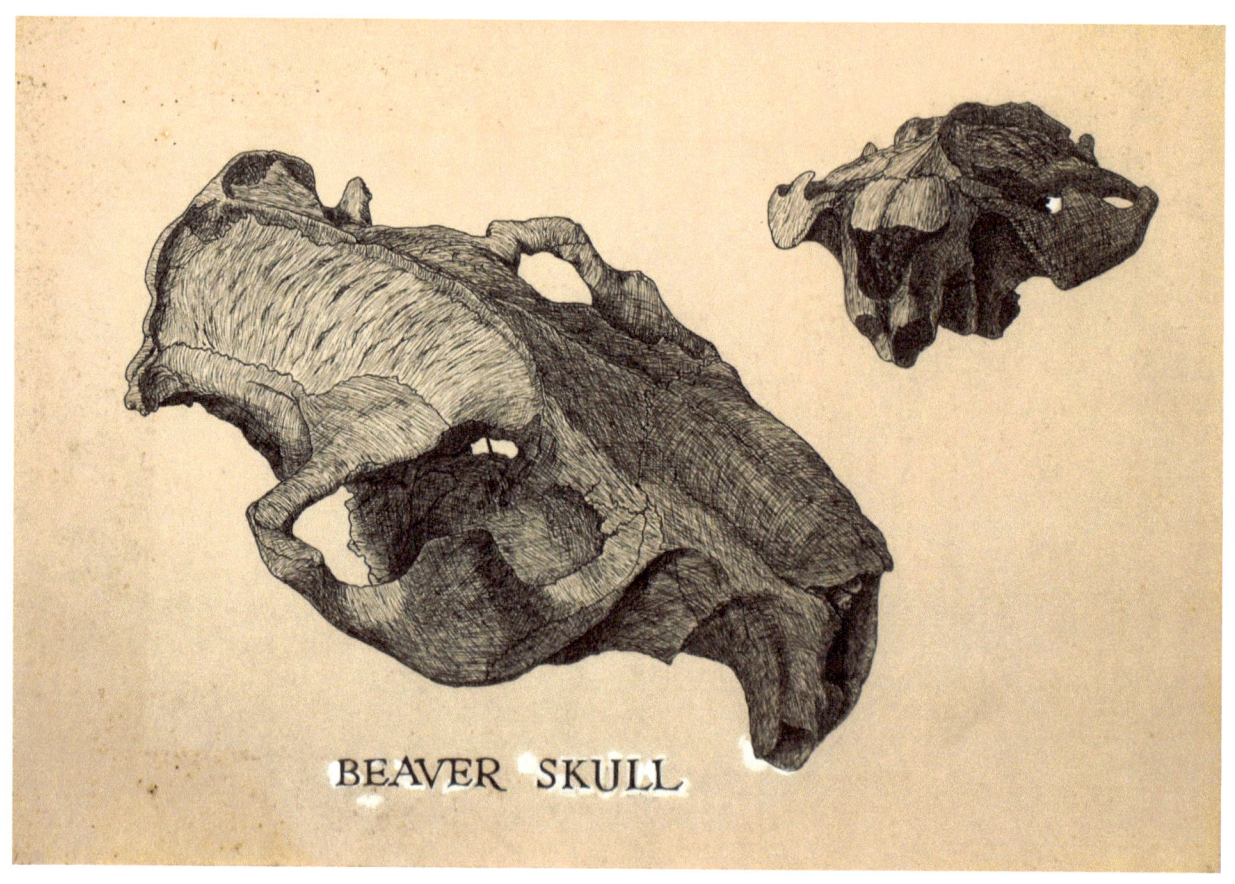

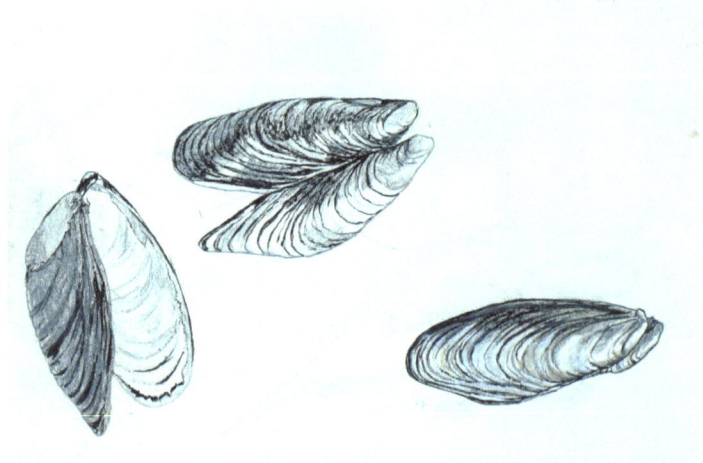

Pen and ink exercises, 1956–1957.

Early Works

Early oil paintings, 1956–1958.

Paintings

When his family lived in Eagle River, Wisconsin, Kauzlaric and his parents attended regular gatherings of artists and writers hosted by Ray and Zola Whitney at their summer home. The first artist Kauzlaric ever met in person was probably illustrator Donn P. Crane. Crane never attained great recognition during his lifetime, but his vibrant, beautifully rendered panels in the My Book House series are classic examples of early twentieth-century illustration. During one of these summer gatherings, Kauzlaric was presented with signed copies of books containing Crane's work. It would be a stretch to say this influenced his work later in life, but meeting someone like Crane and receiving the gift must have made an impression. Kauzlaric glimpsed a world that was possible through art.

The Seattle Art Museum hosted an exhibit of Andrew Wyeth paintings in the early 1970s. Among the many attendees was Kauzlaric, who admired Wyeth immensely. He found himself staring so closely at Wyeth's brushstrokes that he drew the attention of a docent, who politely asked him to maintain a little more distance from the artwork.

Paintings

Opposite: *Donn Crane in his studio, early twentieth century.*

Above, left to right: *Donn Crane, Mrs. Crane, Catherine Kauzlaric, Zola Whitney, Ethel Whitney, Ray Whitney, unknown.*

At the time, Wyeth was one of the few living artists who influenced Kauzlaric's work. Others included Salvador Dali for his surrealistic visions and his lesser-known religious art. A lifelong love of science fiction led him to the work of classic science fiction illustrators like Kelly Freas and John Schoenherr. Freas' work in particular contained a spark of irreverent humor that Kauzlaric appreciated. Humor and symbolism are consistent elements of Kauzlaric's paintings, especially his surreal works.

But, for the most part, Kauzlaric looked to the distant past for artistic role models. He admired Vermeer for his near-perfect portrayals of light, perspective, and texture. Like Vermeer, Kauzlaric never rushed his work. A painting could stay on his easel for years at a time. Like Vermeer, this didn't do a lot to increase Kauzlaric's output over the years. Rembrandt, Hieronymus Bosch, and Holbien were also artists he admired.

Paintings

Whatever brief experiments he did with abstract art in college soon gave way to realism and paintings with solidly classical sensibilities. Kauzlaric looked with disdain on any painting style that lacked, from his perspective, skill in its execution. He definitely saw himself as a nonconformist who was, ironically, committed to doing things traditionally. This could be another reason why he spent so little time in the company of other artists in his early years.

Kauzlaric almost concealed the medium in which he worked. With many of his paintings, one needs to stand quite close to even see his brushstrokes. He wasn't a fan of using large amounts of paint, even on a four-by-eight-foot canvas. He eschewed heavy use of the palette knife and was sparing in the use of large, coarse brushes, except when prepping a canvas. He was more interested in creating an illusion that went from his mind to the viewer's eye without interruption. Consequently, works could remain on his big wall-mounted easel for two or three years. Smaller works and mosaics were also created during these periods, but these ambitious large paintings dominated his workspace and attention.

Once asked if he ever considered using acrylic pigments instead of the oils he preferred, he responded that he liked the time-tested qualities of oil paint, pointing out the still-vibrant colors of works by Raphael or Titian. He said he'd consider using acrylic paints after they'd proven their ability to retain color for a few hundred years.

Brushes and bric-a-brac on Kauzlaric's easel-side table, 2007.

Paintings

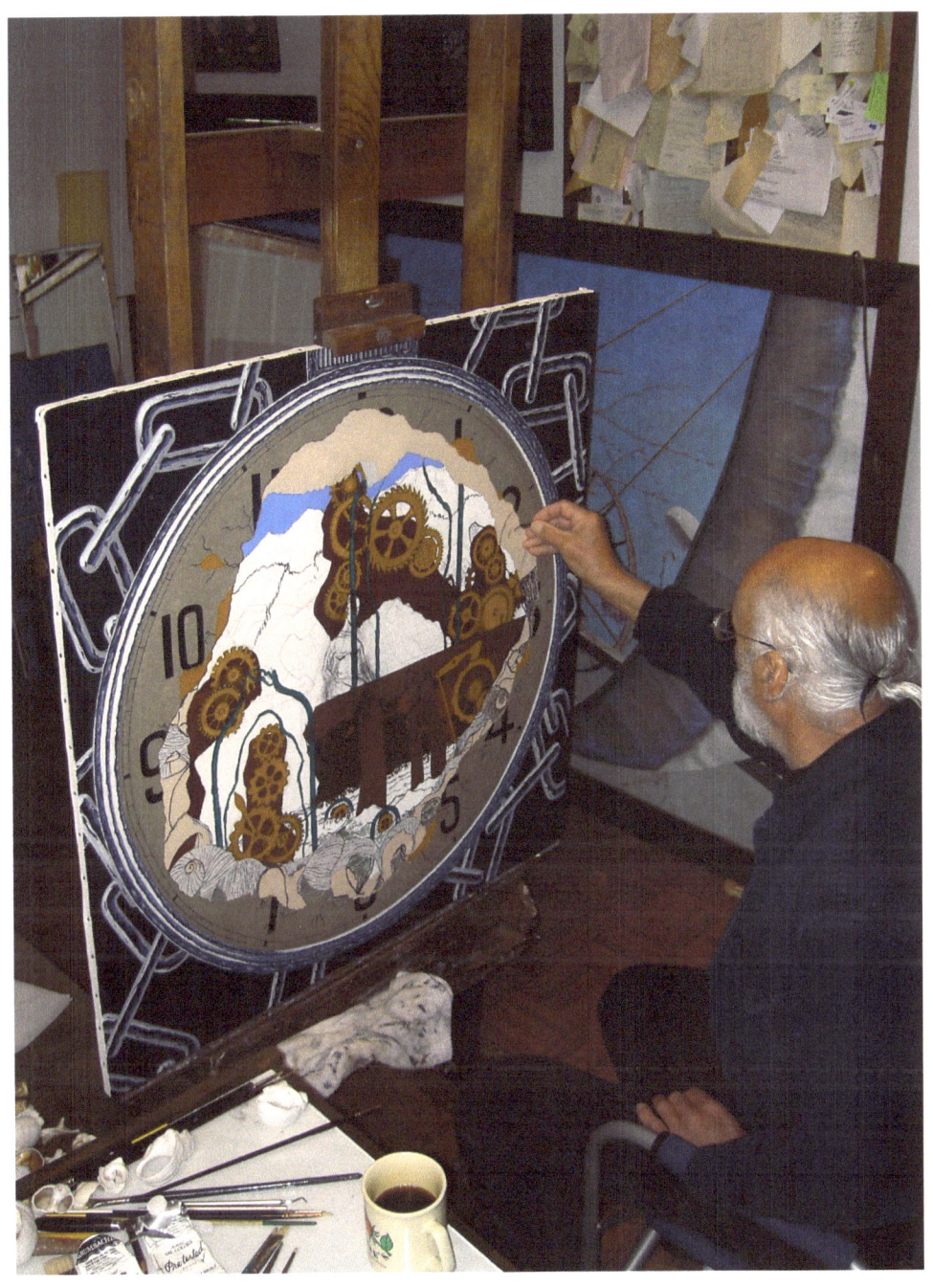

At work on a surrealistic painting with the familiar theme of time, 2005.

Still Life

Above: *Preliminary sketch for Blue Pitcher & Friends, 1973.*

Below: *Blue Pitcher & Friends in progress.*

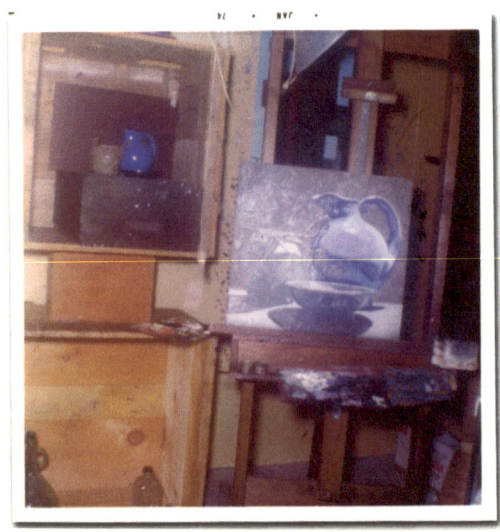

Among the pursuits that drew Kauzlaric as his interest in art took shape were engineering and set design. He said, "I could have been pretty good at stage craft; enough to make a contribution to the art and make a living, but, I couldn't see myself in a theatrical life."

It's hard to say if this were true, but careful staging remained a key aspect of his artwork. His interest in staging and lighting is never more apparent than with his still life paintings. There is a crisp, vivid clarity to the shapes, textures, and forms in these paintings. This isn't an accident. Among the things he designed and constructed for his studio was a light box in which he could control how light fell upon a subject through a number of simple openings. This kept the environment consistent, and it cast the objects into vivid relief. His lighting technique brought out intriguing aspects of texture as well as eccentricities of optics and distortions within glass and reflective surfaces. All this was faithfully rendered by a hand that never quite lost a knack for engineering.

Still Life

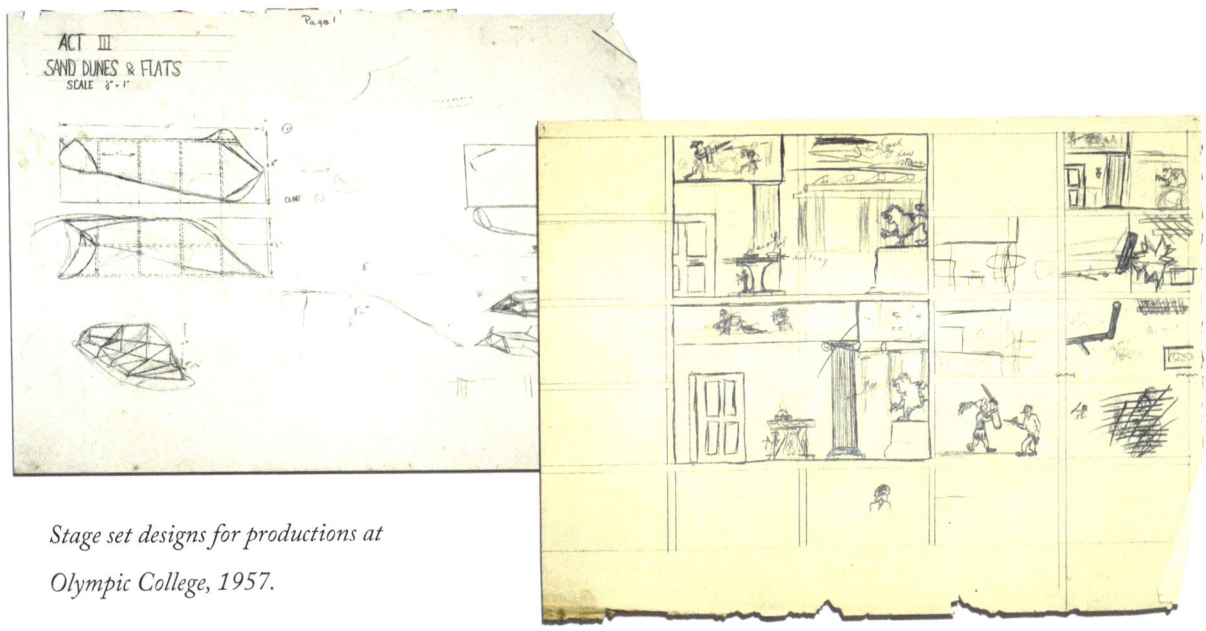

Stage set designs for productions at Olympic College, 1957.

This faithfulness to detail resulted in the only known self-portrait Kauzlaric ever painted. If you look carefully at the reflection of the bowl in the foreground of *Blue Pitcher & Friends* from 1972 (p. 68), it's possible to see a small rendition of his face looking back at you, right where he saw it as he leaned in to look at the scene.

Windfall Apples — *1961* — *The Kauzlaric Art Trust*   *Oil on Masonite*

Still Life

Jug & Bottles — *1967* — Nys Collection

Oil on Masonite

Still Life

Bottles & Coffee Pot — *1972* — *King Collection*   *Oil on Masonite*

Still Life

Copper Coffee Pot & Tape Measure — *1974* — *King Collection* *Oil on Masonite*

Still Life

Skulls — *1969* — *The Kauzlaric Art Trust*

Oil on Masonite

Still Life

Blue Pitcher & Friends — *1973*   *Oil on Masonite*

Still Life

Detail from Blue Pitcher & Friends.

Still Life

Oil Lamps — *1970* — *King Collection* *Oil on brown paper*

Still Life

Oil Lamps — *1972* — King Collection

Oil on brown paper

Still Life

Hazelnuts, a.k.a. Brad's Nuts — *1973* — *Galles Collection*   *Oil on Masonite*

Still Life

Shallots & Canning Jar — *1973* — *Nys Collection* *Oil on Masonite*

Still Life

Dead Man's Chest — 1972 — *Nys Collection*

Oil on Masonite

Opposite: *Detail from* Dead Man's Chest.

Still Life

Decoy & Bottles — *1982* — *Morell Collection* Oil on Masonite

Still Life

Bugle & Cultivator — *1982 — Morell Collection*   *Oil on Masonite*

Still Life

Bottles & Horn — 1979 — *Keagan Kauzlaric Collection*   *Oil on Masonite*

Still Life

Goblet, China & Eggshell — *1980* — *Papineau Collection*   *Oil on Masonite*

Surrealism

Despite the fanciful settings and themes of his surrealistic paintings, the works created while Kauzlaric was still employed as a sanitation worker are nearly always anchored by very real things. The people portrayed are usually friends and relatives, though he sometimes fabricated subjects in his mind's eye. The objects are often things he found and brought home from his day's work on the garbage truck. He dubbed these works "surrealistic still lifes," since they contained both real and imaginary components. This style saw its zenith in *Hiz Honor John Schold* (pp. 96–97), which features one of his lunch counter friends riding a vintage hay rake through the sky.

After Kauzlaric retired from his garbage route, he relied more on settings and subjects drawn completely from his imagination. It's as though the anchor of real objects, places, and people was suddenly gone and less integral to his creative process. The *Channel Marker* paintings are the best example of this.

Kauzlaric's wit is most obvious in his surreal visions. Some carry religious meaning. Others deal with the fragility of time and nature. Visual illusions and outright puns are also common. Some paintings contain all of the above.

Surrealism

Gross Domestic Product — *1969 — Klinton Kauzlaric Collection* *Oil on Masonite*

Surrealism

Fishing Hole — *1974* — *The Kauzlaric Art Trust*   *Oil on Masonite*

Surrealism

Detail from Fishing Hole.

Surrealism

Squeezebox — 1973 — The Kauzlaric Art Trust   *Oil on Masonite*

Surrealism

Photo: Steve Zugschwerdt

Kitsap Sun, Bremerton, Wash., used by permission.

At work on September 34th.

Surrealism

September 34th — *1995* — *The Kauzlaric Art Trust* Oil on canvas

Surrealism

Channel Marker #3 — 1997 — *The Kauzlaric Art Trust* *Oil on canvas*

Surrealism

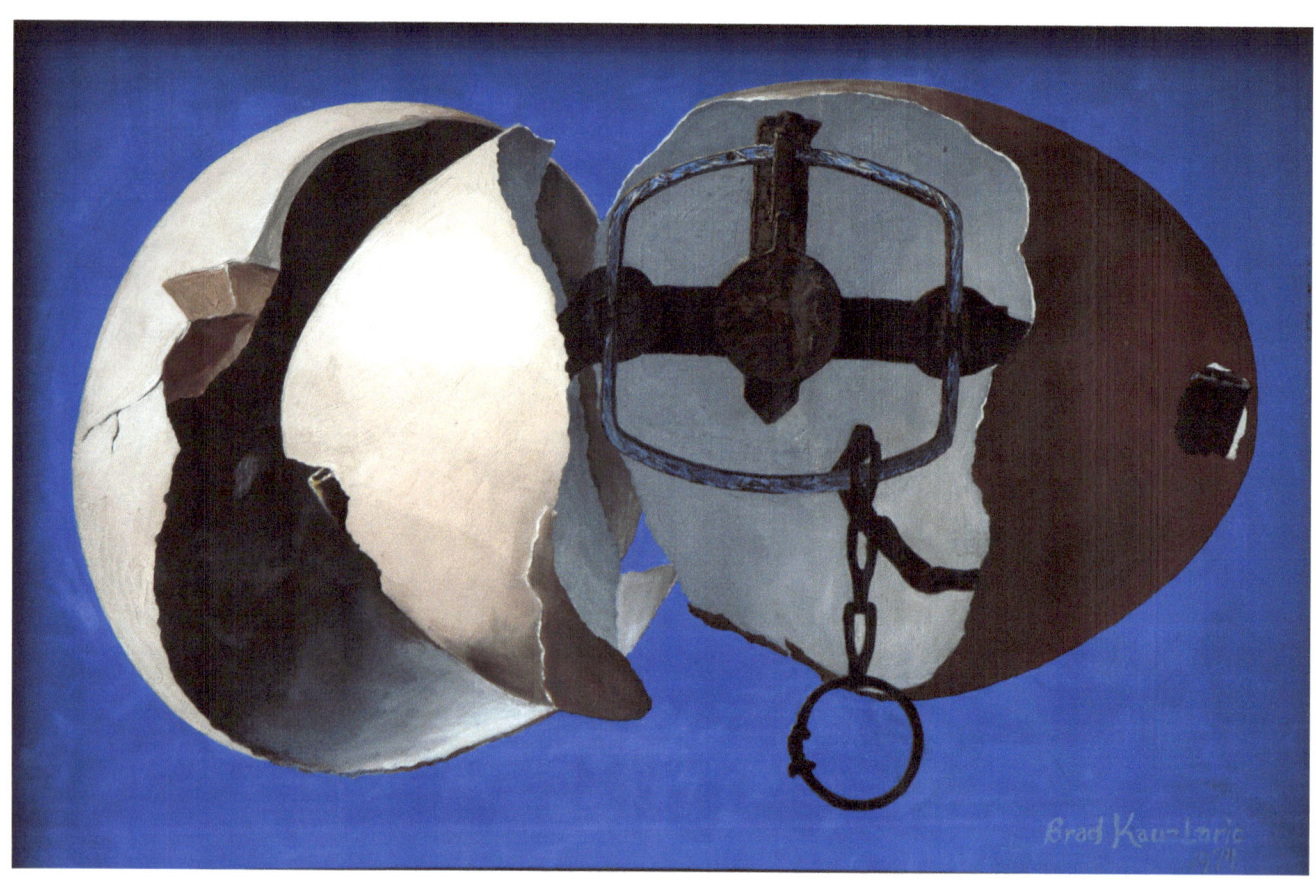

Mother of Invention #1 — *1971 — Clayton Kauzlaric Collection* *Oil on Masonite*

Surrealism

Mother of Invention #2 — *1975 — Ricketts Collection*   *Oil on Masonite*

Surrealism

Nude With Stained Glass — *1983* — *The Kauzlaric Art Trust* *Oil on canvas*

Software — 1983 — The Kauzlaric Art Trust

Oil on canvas

Surrealism

Nude With Moon Snail Shells — *1983* — *The Lyons Collection*   *Oil on canvas*

Hiz Honor John Schold

It started with an old hay rake that was rusting away in a pasture near Silverdale. Kauzlaric probably saw it as he worked his route for Brem-Air Disposal. One day, he was struck by an idea for a painting. It featured a figure riding the old horse-drawn farm equipment, but in his vision, the rake was fitted with sails and flying across the sky. Kauzlaric quickly drew a rough sketch on the back of a handy repair form for his garbage truck.

He chose his old friend John Schold to sit for the role of the flying hay rake's pilot. John was the son of a pioneer family in Kitsap County and a lunch counter pal from Bogard's Drug Store, in Silverdale. John sat a number of times for the painting and was given one of the preliminary studies Kauzlaric used as a reference while working on the painting.

Surrealism

The painting took nearly two years to complete and drew upon every technique Kauzlaric possessed as a painter. The end result is every bit as grand and imposing as he'd hoped and ranks among his finest works. It is a testament to his artistic skill, his love of local history, and his friendship with (Hiz Honor) John Schold.

Opposite: *Kauzlaric in his studio during the production of* Hiz Honor John Schold.

Above right: *John Schold sitting for the painting.*

Lower right: T*he preliminary sketch used as reference for the larger rendition.*

Surrealism

Hiz Honor John Schold — *1983 to 1985* — *The Kauzlaric Art Trust*

Surrealism

Oil on canvas

Surrealism

ART BRIEFS

Painting portrays Silverdale pioneer

When he was growing up on a Silverdale farm, John Schold would have given anything for a sailing hayrake. Farming was hard work.

Seabeck artist Brad Kauzleric dreamed up the sailpowered contraption for his portrait of the Central Kitsap son of a pioneer family.

The four-by-eight-foot surreal oil painting will be on public display throughout February at Silverdale State Bank, 9490 Silverdale Way. It pictures a round genial man in gray hair and striped overalls holding the rake rudder in one hand and the line in the other.

The painting is Kauzleric's way of telling the story of Schold's family.

From his childhood in the 1920s, Schold remembers the smell of homemade lye soap on his grandmother's hands, delivering piglets to the Camp Union logging operation with his father, and delivering vegetables, meat and eggs around Hood Canal.

He gradually eased out of the dairy business and into high-tech excavation when he bought a secondhand backhoe to dig ditches and clear land. Now he runs diesel shovels on a laser-guidance system.

All Schold lacks is a real sailing hayrake for sky-tending chores.

The Seattle Times

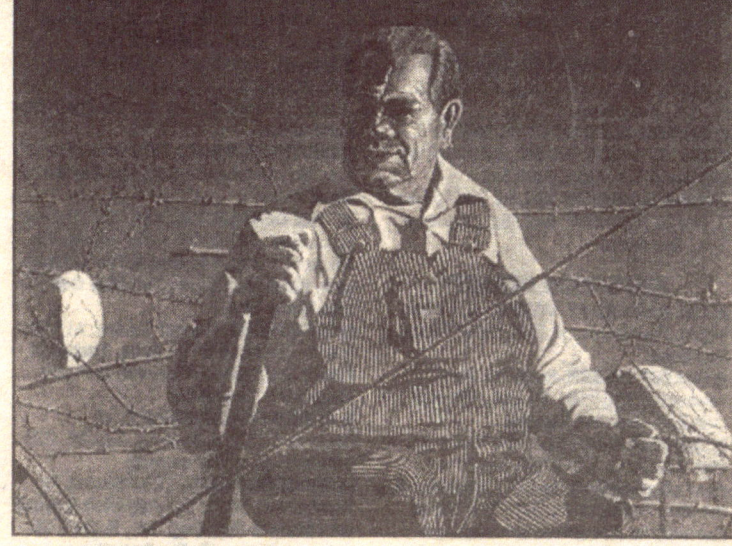

FLYING FARMER: *In a detail from Brad Kauzleric's painting, John Schold navigates a flying hay rake.*

HizHonor John Schold by Seabeck artist Brad Kauzlaric

Kauzlaric Painting On Display

HizHonor John Schold, a 48"x96" oil painting by Brad Kauzlaric of Seabeck, will be on display during the month of February during regular business hours at Silverdale State Bank, 9490 Silverdale Way N.W., Silverdale.

John Schold of Silverdale, depicted in the surreal painting, is the grandson of one of the first Silverdale-Clear Creek homesteading families. His life has reflected the many changes in this area, a story of tremendous growth and conversion.

The only other public exhibition of this work was at the Lawson Gallery in Seattle last year as part of Kauzlaric's one-man retrospective show.

"I think the Seattle market may not identify with the themes in this painting. It is a large work; but it is more," says Kauzlaric. "Over the years I have known John Schold, he has shared some of his memories about the Schold family history that began in 1896 when his grandfather, Andrew, came to Silverdale from San Francisco. This painting is the result of my opportunity to record a portion of this story, one of stuggle and human adaptability. Naturally, I tell it in my fashion — visually."

Kitsap Sun, Bremerton, Wash., used by permission.

Opposite: *Details from* Hiz Honor John Schold.

Above: *Newspaper clippings about the painting.*

Surrealism

Detail from Hiz Honor John Schold.

Surrealism

The Hands of Time — *1983* — *The Kieffer Collection* *Oil on canvas*

Surrealism

Channel Marker #1— *1996 — The Kauzlaric Art Trust* *Oil on canvas*

Surrealism

Channel Marker #2— *1997 — The Kauzlaric Art Trust* *Oil on canvas*

The Tree Series

Kauzlaric's business cards once included the phrase "Architectural Accessories." He applied this definition to stained glass windows, carvings, mosaics, and other works that might embellish a home. It's easy to see how these paintings might be a part of that category. He saw the paintings in this series as something that would easily integrate with the interiors of Northwest buildings and homes. He also had hopes that the tree paintings would find an audience due to their simple, accessible nature.

There is an elemental quality to these works that makes them stand out from his complex surrealistic paintings, and the varied tones and textures of his still life paintings. Trees appear in other works, but in this series they are rendered with stark simplicity, thrown against a backdrop of typically flat, gray Pacific Northwest skies. The limbs are unadorned, barren and leafless, though many contain the leaf buds of early spring.

The tree paintings were created over a twelve-year period and comprise Kauzlaric's most long-running and cohesive series of paintings.

The Tree Series

Apple Tree — *1982 — Alicia Payne Collection* *Oil on canvas*

The Tree Series

Scrub Alders #1 — *1989 — The Kauzlaric Art Trust* *Oil on Masonite*

The Tree Series

Scrub Alders #2 — *1989 — Kauzlaric Art Trust* *Oil on Masonite*

The Tree Series

Scrub Alders #3 — *1989 — The Kauzlaric Art Trust*

Oil on Masonite

Alders — *1982 — Nelson Collection*

Oil on Masonite

The Tree Series

Pearlace — 1978 — *The Kauzlaric Art Trust* *Oil on Masonite*

The Tree Series

Alder Lace — *1989 — The Kauzlaric Art Trust*

The Tree Series

Oil on canvas

The Tree Series

The Foolish Virgins — *1980* — *Clayton Kauzlaric Collection*

The Tree Series

Oil on Masonite

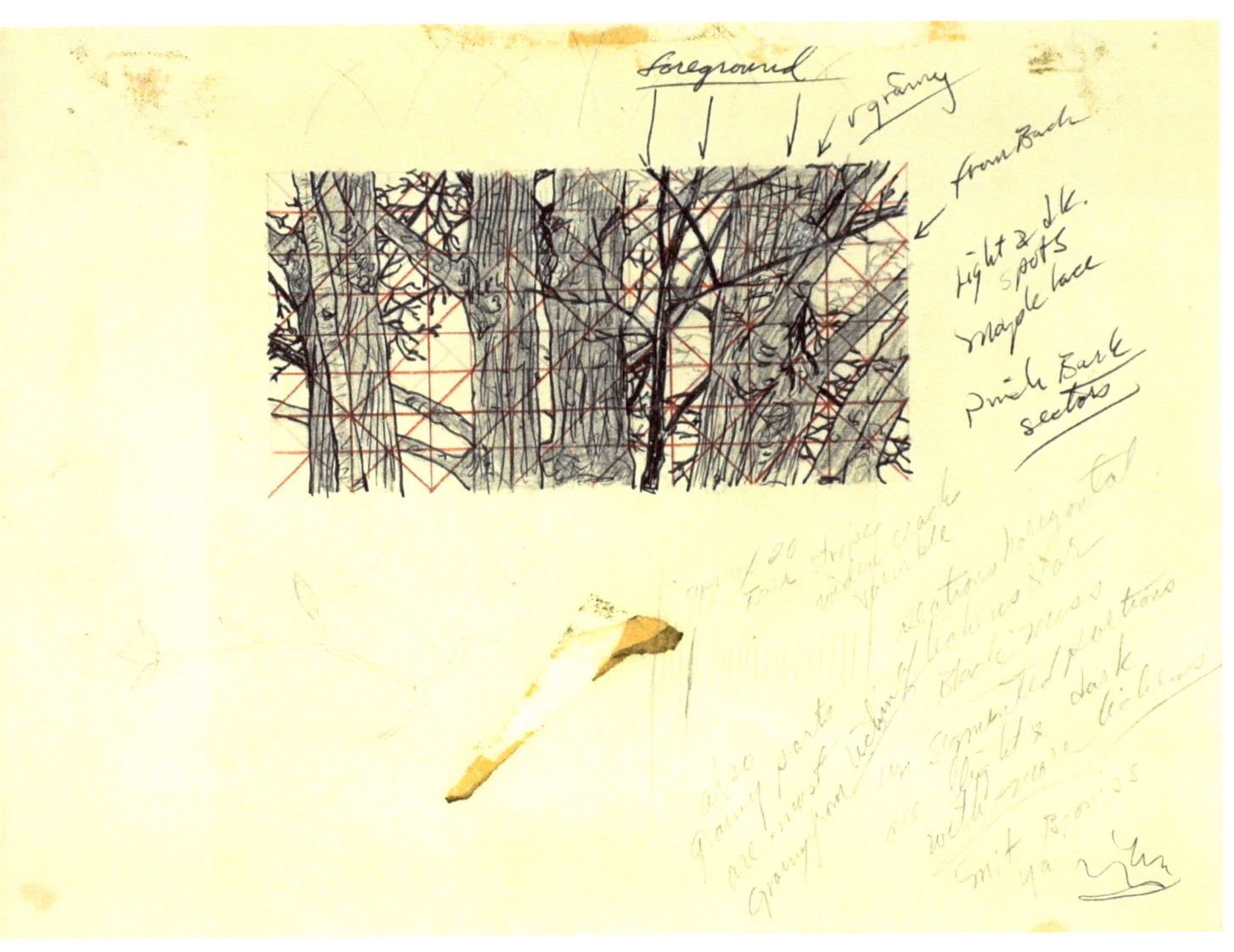

Above: *Preliminary sketch and notes for* The Foolish Virgins.

Opposite: *Detail from* The Foolish Virgins.

Portraits

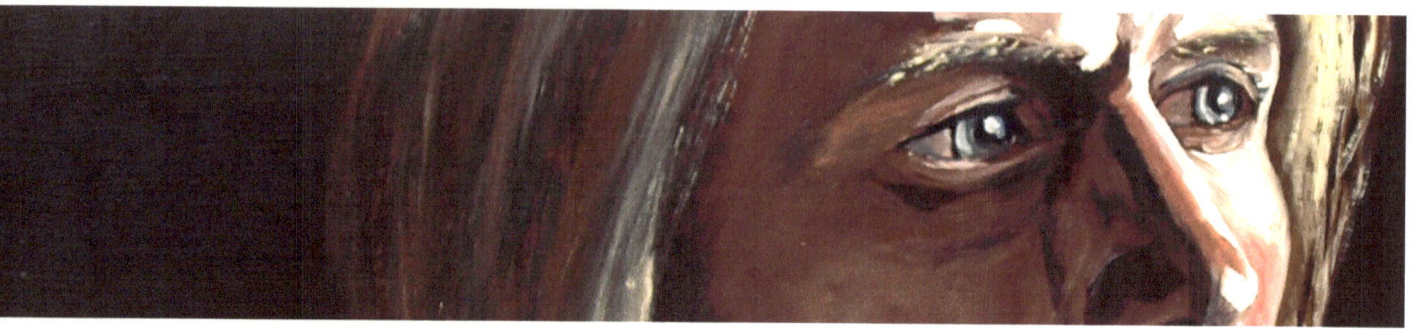

Portraits weren't a major aspect of Kauzlaric's artwork, but those he did were usually of people who mattered to him. Most are of close friends, family, and people he encountered during the course of his day's work. Kauzlaric's wife, DeAnna, has the distinction of being one of a few people who were painted more than once. The others were Kauzlaric's friend Bill King and work associate Jackie Lyons. Kauzlaric's mother-in-law, Ferne Johnson, was always convinced that *Gross Domestic Product* (p. 81) was of her mother, Travilla.

Real individuals figure in many of Kauzlaric's paintings, particularly his surrealistic pieces, with *Hiz Honor John Schold* (p. 96) being the best example.

As with other natural subjects, Kauzlaric thought in terms of the architecture of every face he painted and the history they contained. He lavished many hours on the *Portrait of Anne Mata* (p. 119), intrigued by the thought that her features were reminiscent of ancient Mayan carvings.

Portraits

Young African American — *1957* — *The Kauzlaric Art Trust*　　　*Oil on art board*

But his penchant for careful planning and execution sometimes eclipsed the facial expressions and warmer qualities of his subjects. The results could be, at times, a little stiff and lifeless. The careful analysis that worked well for painting a bowl or a frayed length of rope didn't always succeed as well where a human was concerned.

Portraits

Elderly Woman — *1957* — *The Kauzlaric Art Trust* *Oil on art board*

Portraits

Arnold Wang — *1967 — Wang Family Collection* *Oil on canvas*

Portraits

Ann Mata — *1969* — *The Kauzlaric Art Trust*　　　　　　　　　　*Oil on Masonite*

Portraits

Zillah Jones — *1972* — *The Kauzlaric Art Trust*   *Oil on Masonite*

Portraits

Bill King — *1974* — *King Collection*   *Oil on Masonite*

Portraits

Nude — *1983* — *The Kauzlaric Art Trust*   *Oil on canvas*

Portraits

John Hoover — *2003* — *Hoover Collection*   *Oil on canvas*

Mosaics

First mosaic, 1957.

Kauzlaric's mosaics are arguably his most distinctive work. He developed a style and production methodology that distinguishes them in a number of ways. His extensive use of native materials from local beaches gives them a unique tone and texture. Found materials were also incorporated when conventional materials lacked a specific color he was looking for.

Kauzlaric's early mosaics were capably done, but most were basically pictures made of tiles. As he gained confidence and expertise in the medium, he created more complex, engaging images. The best of his mosaics have an illusion of depth achieved with varying amounts of reflectivity and negative space. Depending on the lighting and time of day, these mosaics have a real sense of movement, like a school of fish swimming through sunlit water beneath a pier. Indigenous materials from Northwest beaches, notably clam and mussel shells, added more texture and visual interest while framing the vibrant colors of the glass with their neutral, earthy tones.

Mosaics

Photo Jo Albertson, 1991.

Early themes ranged from nautical subject matter such as ships, fish, and compasses, to animals, including a mural of buffalo and an American eagle. There are works depicting pitchers, fruit, and bottles. Nautical subjects eventually became a dominant theme. The sophistication of how he layered and structured images reached his most distinctive style with *Perch* in 1969 (p. 135). This approach eventually found its way to larger works such as *Shrimp Pot* in 1993 (p. 139), culminating in the much larger *Perch & Pilings* in 2003 (pp. 142–143). This last large mosaic is currently housed at the Marine Science Center in Poulsbo, Washington.

But by the late 1970s, most of his mosaics focused on sea life and floral representations. Devotional art remained an important priority as well.

His mosaic panels are extremely well made. Kauzlaric was a meticulous planner who believed in making things to last. He was firmly convinced that future generations would naturally want to see his art, so he built accordingly. The strength and durability of his mosaics would be both good and bad as far as posterity is concerned. Some works, including his first efforts on a large mural he made under the tutelage of instructor Hank Blass, were dismantled when new construction loomed. Others, including two large sea horses he did for a hotel at Ocean Shores, Washington, were likely demolished when the building was remodeled. Installing a large mosaic is time-consuming and expensive, and taking one down is even more so. The very quality of permanence that Kauzlaric sought cut both ways. (See also *Missing Works*, p. 204.)

Opposite top: *Kauzlaric learned mosaic making techniques while studying with Hank Blass. He assisted in the construction of* The Progress of Man *during his student years at Olympic College.*

Opposite bottom: *An early mosaic of a guitar, bottle and fruit.*

Above: Perch & Pilings *in progress.*

Mosaics

Pitcher & Oranges — *1965* — *Klinton Kauzlaric Collection*

Mosaics

Buffalo — *1968* — *The Lindgren Collection*

Mosaics

Madronas — *1958* — *The Kauzlaric Art Trust*

Mosaics

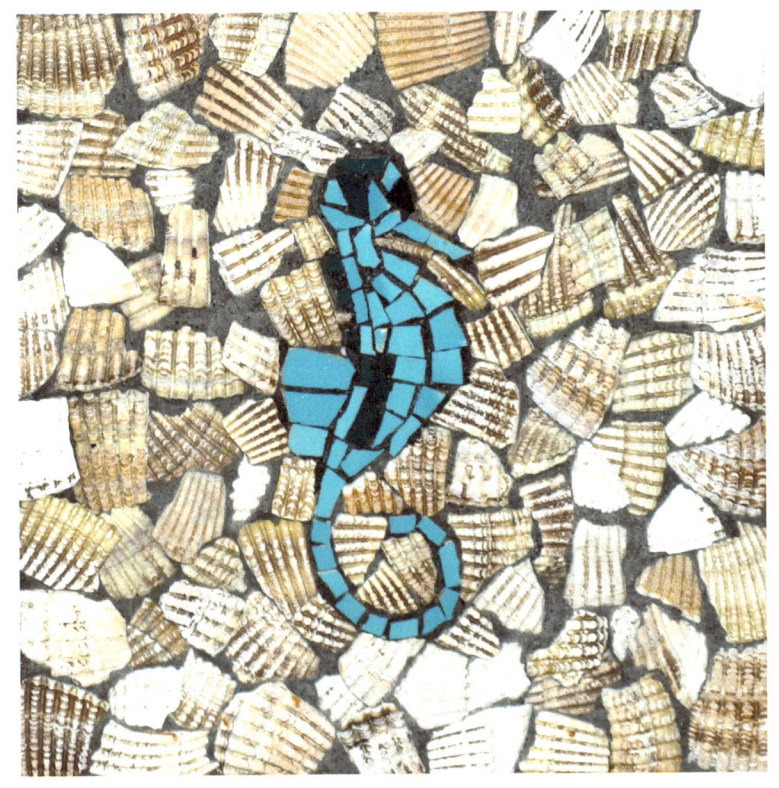

Sea Horses — *1965 — Ashley Kauzlaric Collection*

Mosaics

Ship & Compass — *1966* — *Proteau Collection*

Mosaics

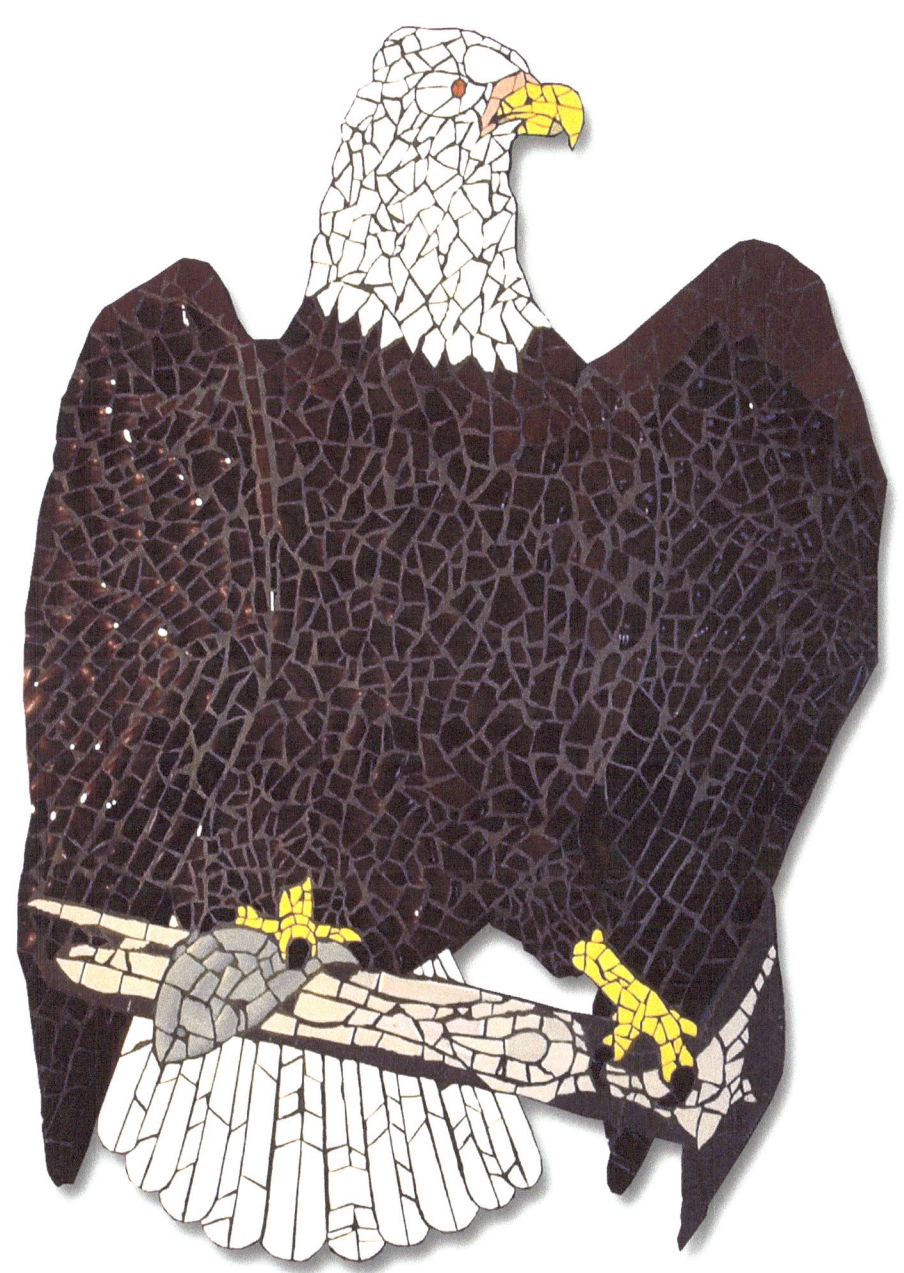

Eagle's Rest — *1971* — *Papineau Collection*

Mosaics

Marine Life — *1967* — *The Kauzlaric Art Trust*

Mosaics

Perch — *1969* — *The Kauzlaric Art Trust*

Mosaics

Fishnet — *1971 — Singer Collection*

Mosaics

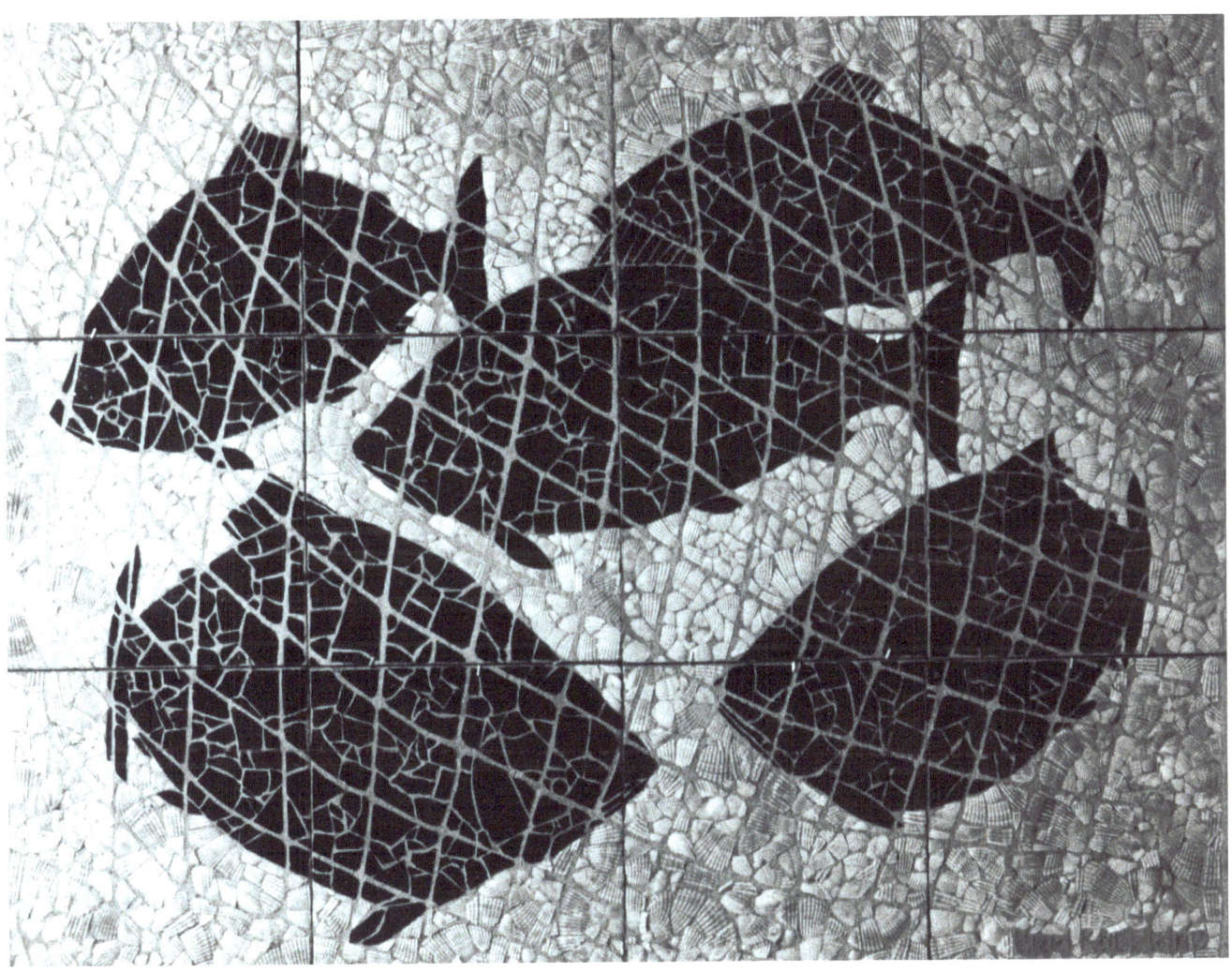

Fishnet 2 — *1999*

Mosaics

Starry Flounder Left-Eyed — *2006* — *The Kauzlaric Art Trust*

Mosaics

Shrimp Pot — *1978 — The Kauzlaric Art Trust*

Mosaics

Three Starfish — *1998* — *The Kauzlaric Art Trust*

Mosaics

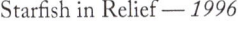

Starfish Panel —*1999* — *The Kauzlaric Art Trust*

Starfish in Relief — *1996*

The Kauzlaric Art Trust

141

Perch & Pilings — *2003— Poulsbo Marine Science Center*

Mosaics

Holy Flounder — *1999—Arness Collection*

Mosaics

Details from Holy Flounder.

Mosaics

Winter Garden—*2004*

Daisies on Black—*2005*

The Kauzlaric Art Trust

Daisies — *2001* — *The Kauzlaric Art Trust*

Mosaics

Two Crabs —*1993*— *The Kauzlaric Art Trust*

Devotional Works

Below: *Kauzlaric with the* Stella Maris *mosaic, 1998*

Kauzlaric was raised as a Roman Catholic, but his parents' frequent moves around the country made it difficult for him to consider any one church his home until his family moved to Bremerton. He attended the early fisherman's mass at Our Lady Star of the Sea while he was in high school, his regular attendance sometimes interrupted by weekends spent fishing and hiking.

Local Catholic parishes were a source of several commissions. When Holy Trinity Parish in Bremerton was constructed in the late 1960s, Kauzlaric undertook the creation of its *Stations of the Cross* (pp. 151–164). He took a rare leave of absence from his job at Brem-Air Disposal in 1968 and spent six weeks producing a series of fourteen mosaics. This set represents the largest series of images he ever created. He later produced six mosaic holy water fonts for Our Lady Star of the Sea parish in 1971 (p. 165).

Kauzlaric wanted to create a life-size portrayal of the Virgin Mary for a number of years. His *Stella Maris* mosaic (p. 166) embodies both his personal faith and his love of nature. He donated the Madonna to Our Lady Star of the Sea parish days before his death in

Devotional Works

5th Station — *1974* *Holy Trinity Parish,*

2007. It was installed at the Stella Maris women's shelter on his birthday in 2010, and dedicated to his parents, Jake and Catherine Kauzlaric.

Some of Kauzlaric's works that aren't overtly religious contain religious symbolism. *Witness* is a good example of this (p. 173). In terms of technical execution, this ranks among his most visually intricate works. The window of the old house contains incredible detail, including a completely legible coffee can hidden under layers of obscuring paint. When it was suggested that adding such detail only to cover it with paint was pointless, Kauzlaric replied "Yes—but I know it's there." The old kite in the tree is a subtle cruciform. One can only speculate on the meaning Kauzlaric placed on such symbolism, but these elements clearly developed some importance to him over the countless hours he spent in front of his easel.

Devotional Works

Station 1: Jesus is Condemned to Death

Holy Trinity Parish,

Devotional Works

Station 2: Jesus Carries His Cross

Holy Trinity Parish

Devotional Works

Station 3: Jesus Falls the First Time

Holy Trinity Parish

Devotional Works

Station 4: Jesus Meets His Mother

Holy Trinity Parish

Devotional Works

Station 5: Simon of Cyrene helps Jesus Carry the Cross

Holy Trinity Parish

Devotional Works

Station 6: Veronica Wipes the Face of Jesus *Holy Trinity Parish*

Devotional Works

Station 7: Jesus Falls the Second Time

Holy Trinity Parish

Devotional Works

Station 8: Jesus Meets the Women of Jerusalem

Holy Trinity Parish

Devotional Works

Station 9: Jesus Falls the Third Time

Holy Trinity Parish

Devotional Works

Station 10: Jesus is Stripped of his Garments

Holy Trinity Parish

Devotional Works

Station 11: Jesus is Nailed to the Cross
Holy Trinity Parish

Devotional Works

Station 12: Jesus Dies on the Cross

Holy Trinity Parish

Devotional Works

Station 13: Jesus is Taken Down from the Cross

Holy Trinity Parish

Devotional Works

Station 14: Jesus is Laid in the Tomb

Holy Trinity Parish

Devotional Works

Holy water font — *1971* *Our Lady Star of the Sea Parish*

Devotional Works

Stella Maris — *1997* Our Lady Star of the Sea Parish

Buildings & Landscapes

Below: *Polaroid reference photo for a decaying barn in Kitsap County, 1970.*

There was a crumbling Victorian house not far from the Kauzlaric home in Brownsville. In the yard surrounding the old house was a collection of wrecked cars, including an old school bus, which was overgrown with blackberry bushes.

This was the Huey house. Both Kauzlaric and his wife, DeAnna, sketched the decaying bus, and Kauzlaric revisited the site years later to create a visual record of the house shortly before it was demolished to make way for a subdivision. The Huey house never appeared in a painting, but the notes and sketches (1987, pp. 176–179) show Kauzlaric's attention to detail and appreciation for the craftsmanship of a bygone era. He calls out materials and techniques used when the house was first built in the margins of these images.

Buildings & Landscapes

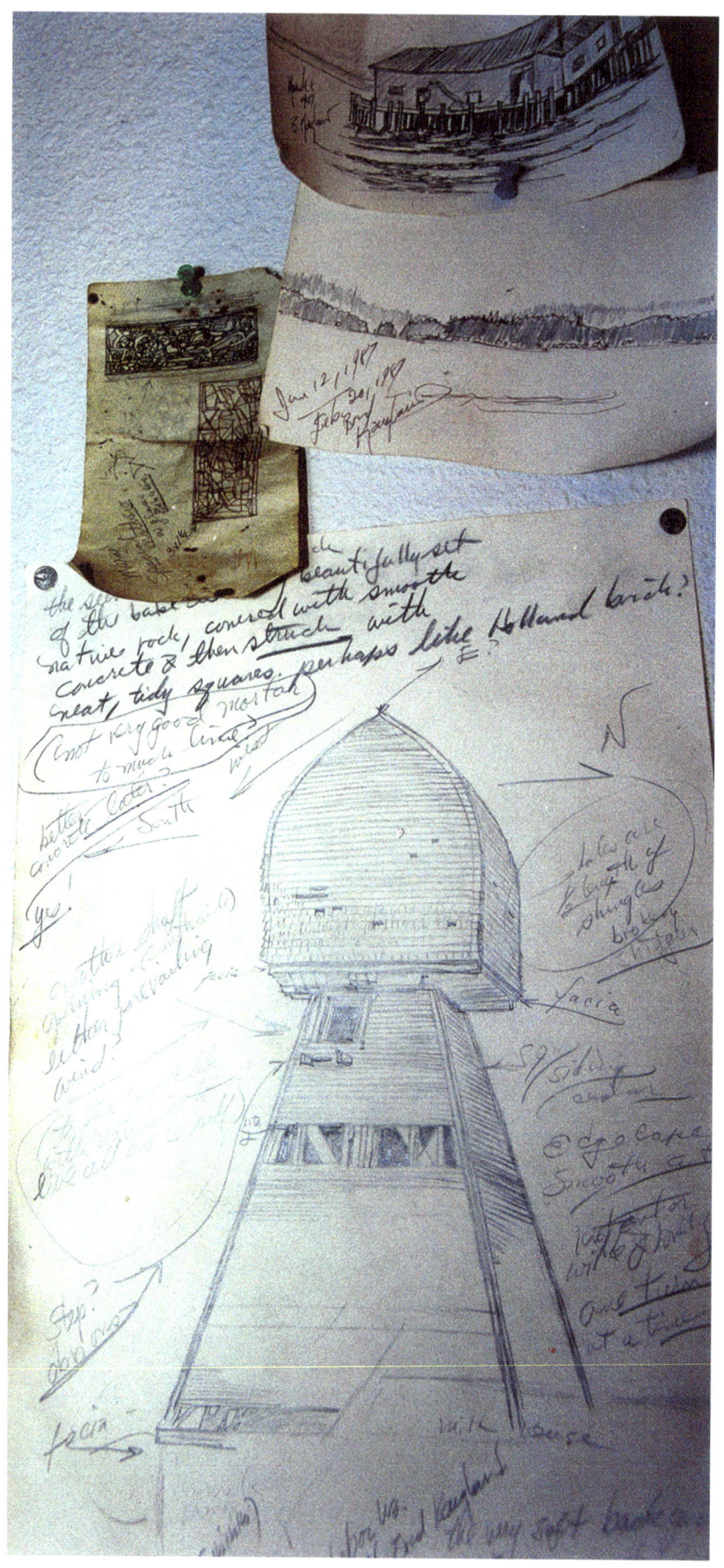

Buildings & Landscapes

Kitsap County locations and buildings appear in a number of Kauzlaric's works, usually as a backdrop or a setting that was altered and folded into a painting's overall concept. Specific real-life details—like the rusting hay rake in *Hiz Honor John Schold* (1983–85, p. 96), the view across Hood Canal to the Dosewallops in *September 34th* (1995, p. 86), the lonely old house in *Witness* (1971, p. 173), and the stand of maple trees in *Foolish Virgins* (1980, pp. 112–113)—were incorporated into paintings. Even surrealistic vistas were usually rooted in local scenery at some level.

Straight landscapes were less common. The few Kauzlaric did are telling. They illustrate what he found intriguing and worthwhile. He was acutely aware of the changes happening to the landscape of Kitsap County. These pieces document aging buildings shortly before their destruction and settings that have since been paved to make way for new houses and shopping malls.

Top and bottom: *A barn built by Kauzlaric with the help of his family at their Gilberton home in 1972. The barn was a compact 12-by-12 feet and made from reclaimed lumber salvaged from a Navy dump.*

Opposite: *Sketches and notes from Kauzlaric's studio wall, 1988.*

Barns were a favorite subject. Kauzlaric's years spent on a farm made him acutely aware of the building traditions behind different barn configurations, and the fact that these techniques were often handed down from one generation of builders to the next. He was concerned about this lore and expertise being lost to future generations. The barns shown here have all been torn down. One used to stand on the current site of the Kitsap Mall in Silverdale, Washington.

Buildings & Landscapes

Kitsap Barn #1 — *1970* — *The King Collection* *Oil on brown paper*

Buildings & Landscapes

Kitsap Barn #2 — *1970* — *The King Collection*　　　　　　　　　　　　　　　　　*Oil on brown paper*

Buildings & Landscapes

Kitsap Barn #3 — *1970* — *The King Collection*　　　　　　　　　　　　　　　　　　　　　　　　　*Oil on brown paper*

Buildings & Landscapes

Witness — 1971 — The Kauzlaric Art Trust   *Oil on Masonite*

Overleaf: *Detail from Witness*

Buildings & Landscapes

Abandoned Bus — *1971* — *The Kauzlaric Art Trust* — *Pastels and ink on paper*

Huey House North Side — *1987* — *The Kauzlaric Art Trust* — *Pen and ink*

Buildings & Landscapes

Huey House North Side 2 — *The Kauzlaric Art Trust* Pen and ink

Buildings & Landscapes

Huey House Roof & Cornice Details — *1987* — The Kauzlaric Art Trust *Pen, ink, and pencil*

Old Kitsap Barn — *1987* — The Kauzlaric Art Trust *Pen, ink, and pencil*

Buildings & Landscapes

Huey House Entryway — *1987* — *The Kauzlaric Art Trust* — *Pen, ink, and pencil*

Sculpture & Other Media

Kauzlaric had a pervasive curiosity about how things are made. He was always devising construction techniques for sculptures, mobiles, and media that ranged far from his core works in oil paints and mosaic. The underlying engineering was always a puzzle he loved, and he applied this combination of creative ideas and practical construction to concepts that never made it off the drawing board, or out of his head for that matter. These ideas ranged from wind-powered sculptures that would play music to fanciful lighter-than-air ships built of glass.

Kauzlaric produced a small number of sculptures. Most of the works were made to satisfy his curiosity. He also created maquettes for several commercial works, but he never succeeded in securing a commission for a substantial project. There are only a few small carvings, some plaster tests, and other bits and pieces that show a mind that was always weighing the logistics of bringing tangible shape and form to the imaginary.

Concrete window installed at the home of Bill and Laura King in Bremerton, Washington, 1975. Small squares of mirror set in the inner frame reflected daylight through the colored glass into the house's interior.

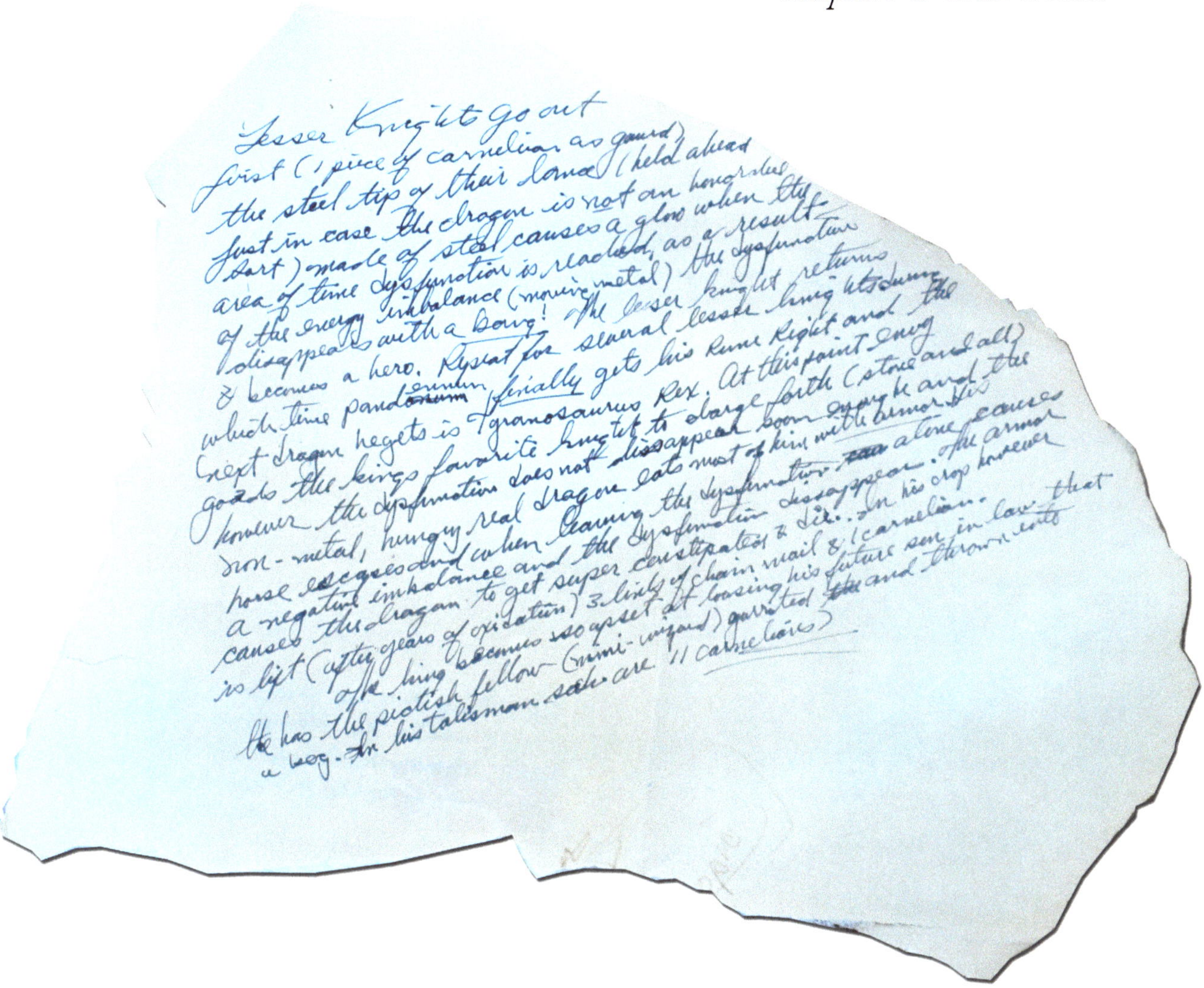

Lesser Knight go out
first (1 piece of carnelian as guard)
the steel tip of their lance (held ahead
just in case the dragon is not an hourglass
dart) made of steel causes a glow when the
area of time dysfunction is reached, as a result
of the energy imbalance (moving metal) the dysfunction
disappears with a bang! The lesser knight returns
& becomes a hero. Repeat for several lesser knights during
which time pandemonium finally gets his rune right and the
next dragon he gets is Tyranosaurus Rex. At this point king
goads the kings favorite knight to charge forth (stone and all)
however the dysfunction does not disappear. Soon enough and the
non-metal, hungry real dragon eats most of him with armor. His
horse escapes and when leaving the dysfunction alone causes
a negative imbalance and the dysfunction disappear. The armor
causes the dragon to get super constipated & die. In his crop however
is left (after years of oxidation) 3 links of chain mail & 1 carnelian. that
The king becomes so upset at loosing his future son in law
He has the piotish fellow (mini-wizard) garroted and thrown into
a bog. In his talisman sack are 11 carnelians)

Above: *Outline of a story, early 1990's.*

Right: *Laura King inspects the window during its construction, 1975.*

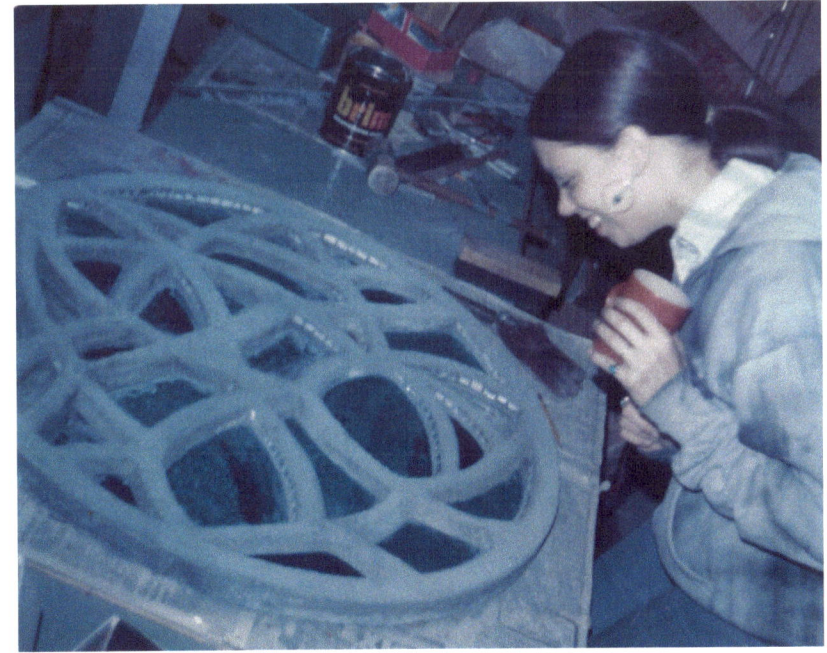

Psyche — 1960 — The Kauzlaric Art Trust   Carved wood

Sculpture & Other Media

Mosaic Eggs — *2007— The Kauzlaric Art Trust* *Glass set in concrete.*

Sculpture & Other Media

Cement windows — 1978 — The Kauzlaric Art Trust

Cement and stained glass

Sculpture & Other Media

Shaman's Eye — *1975* — *The Kauzlaric Art Trust*　　　　　　　　　　　　　　　　*Carved wood*

Northwest Native American motif — *1969* — *The Kauzlaric Art Trust*　　　　　　　*Ink and oils on paper*

Sculpture & Other Media

Northwest Native American placemats — 1970 — Ashley Kauzlaric Collection   *Pen and ink on brown paper*

Top: Eagle — *Bottom:* Moon

Sculpture & Other Media

Top: Mountain Goat — Bottom: Orca

Sculpture & Other Media

Northwest Native American placemats — 1970 — P.R. Hart & Co. *Cut wood photographed and printed on vinyl.*

Top: Eagle — *Bottom:* Moon

Sculpture & Other Media

Top: Mountain Goat — *Bottom:* Orca

The Billygoo Bird — *1997— The Kauzlaric Art Trust* *Oil on canvas*

Unfinished Works

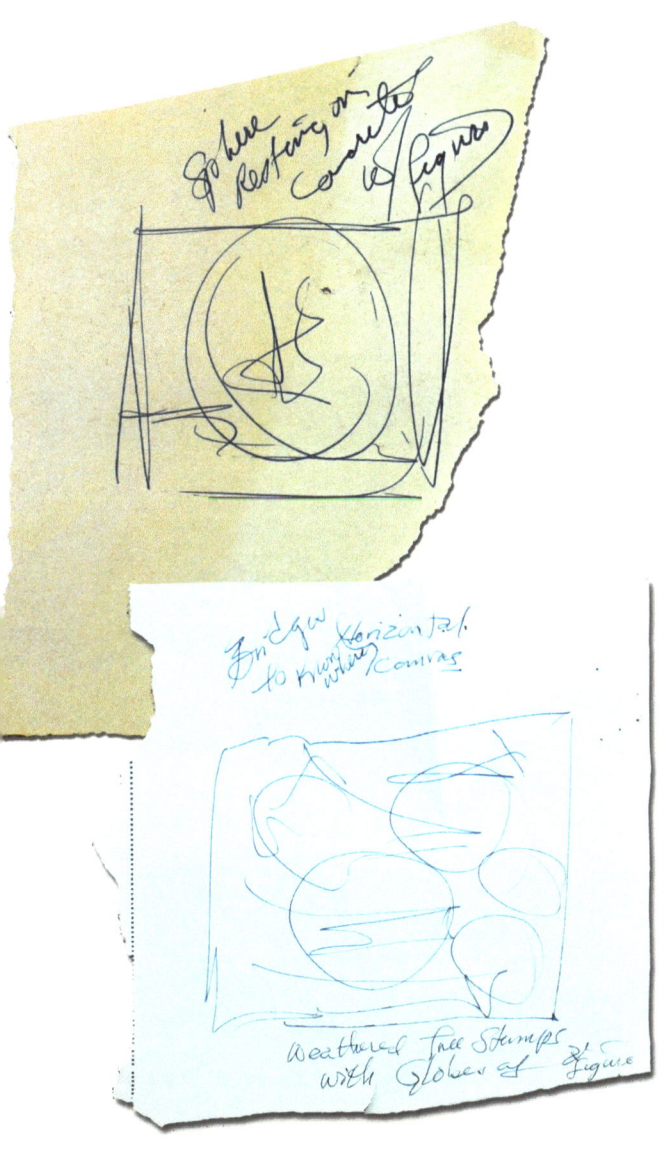

Most creative people leave a trail of unfinished projects and half-considered ideas in their wake. Kauzlaric was no exception. This section includes sketches and samples created to attract commissions, projects that never got off the ground, and rough drawings that never made it to a canvas or a mosaic panel. Many ideas only existed on scraps of paper cluttering the walls and bulletin board in his studios, some of which have been included here. Beyond mock-ups, sketches, and doodles, some ideas were only jotted down as titles for future works:

Asphalt Manor
Pinball
Jack in the Window
Father's Coat
Bumberboom with Wheels
Dante's Refuse Removal
Sherman's Farm
Mossy Triumph with Rust

The titles are tantalizing. What they might have become will never be known.

Unfinished Works

Mobile design—*1967*

The Kauzlaric Art Trust

Watercolor and ink

Marine mosaic design—*1999*

The Kauzlaric Art Trust

Pencil and pastels on paper

Unfinished Works

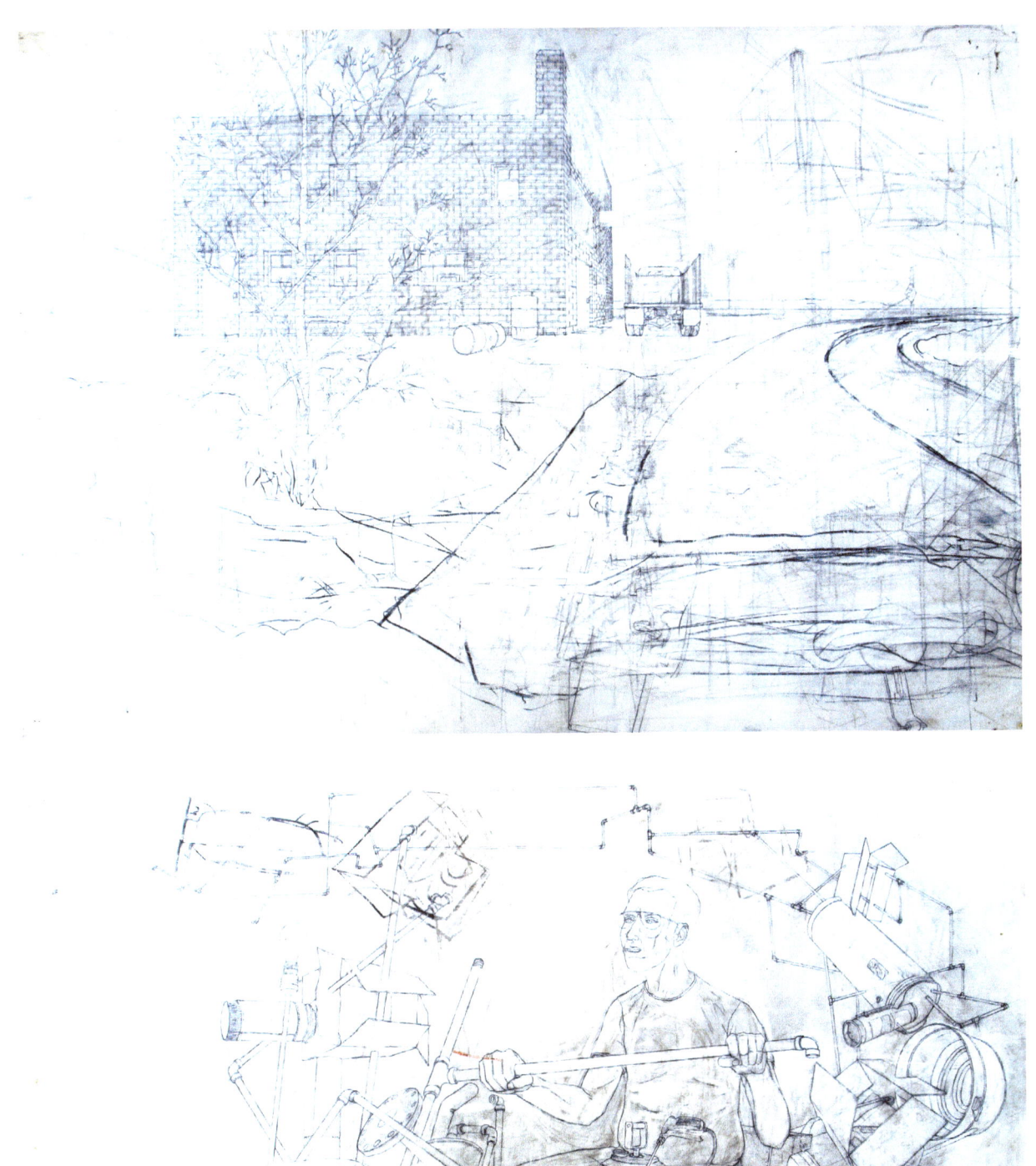

Unfinished paintings — *Late 1960s* — *The Kauzlaric Art Trust*   *Pencil on Masonite*

Unfinished Works

Mosaic proposal & sample panel — *Late 1960s* — *The Kauzlaric Art Trust*   *Watercolor*

Unfinished Works

Unfinished painting — *Late 1960s*

The Kauzlaric Art Trust

Oil on art board

Unfinished Works

Devotional mosaic designs — *Early 1970s* — *The Kauzlaric Art Trust* 　　　　　　　　　　　　　　　　　　　　*Watercolor and ink*

Unfinished Works

Mosaic proposal & sample panel — *Late 1960s* — *The Kauzlaric Art*   *Watercolor and ink*

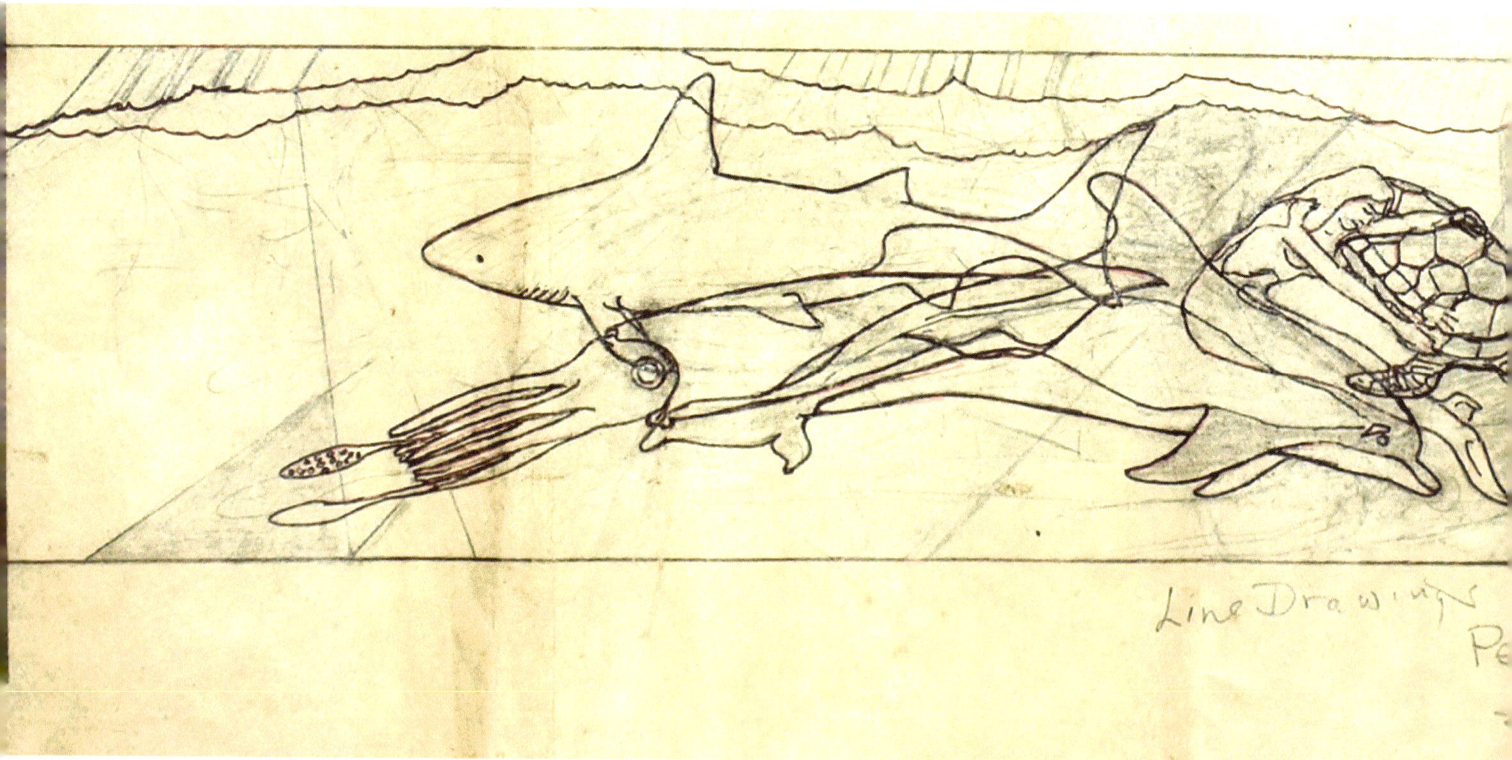

Unfinished Works

Children of the Moon — *Mosaic design* — 1970 — *The Kauzlaric Art Trust*

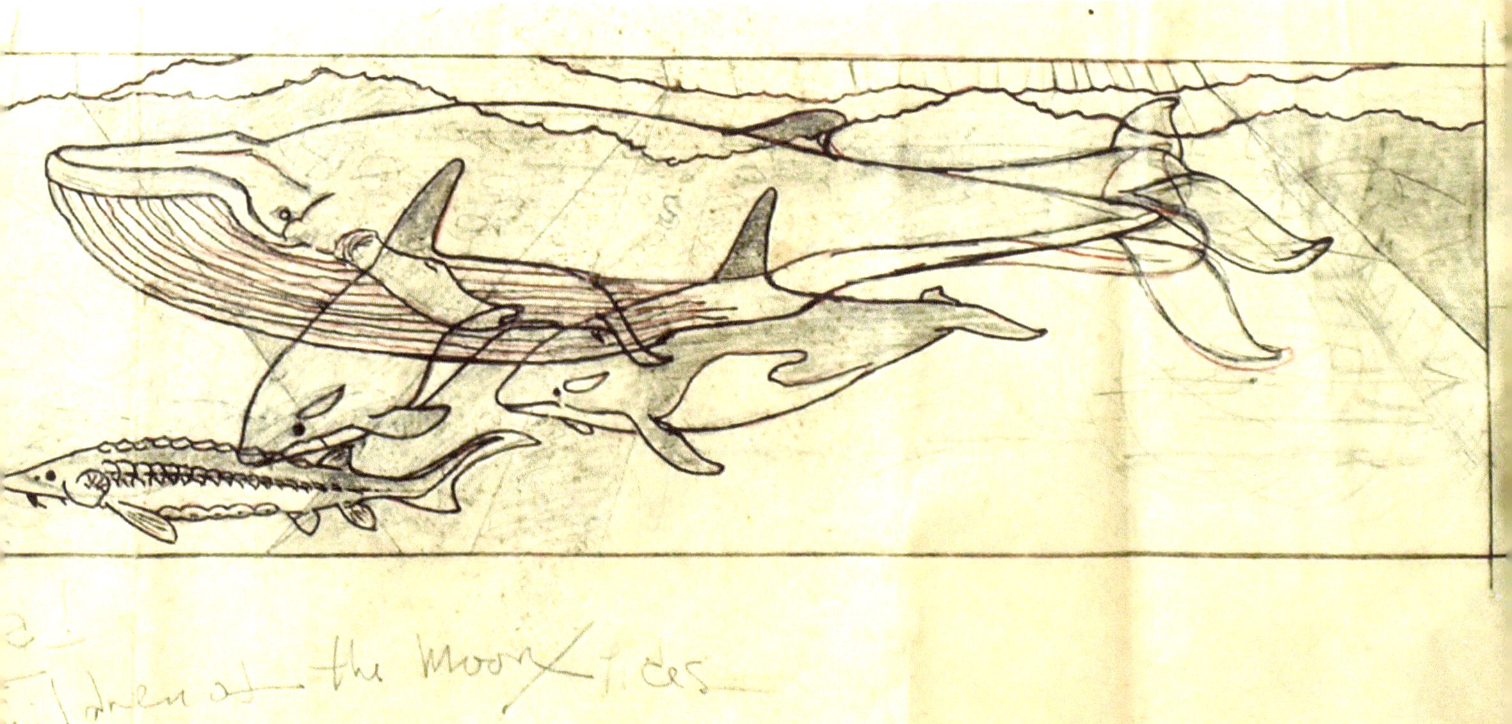

Unfinished Works

Watercolor on paper — Pencil and ink on paper.

Overleaf: *Detail from Children of the Moon*

Unfinished painting — *1990s*
The Kauzlaric Art Trust
Oil on canvas

Unfinished Works

Salmon mosaic design — *2005* — *The Kauzlaric Art Trust* *Pastels and ink on paper*

Unfinished Works

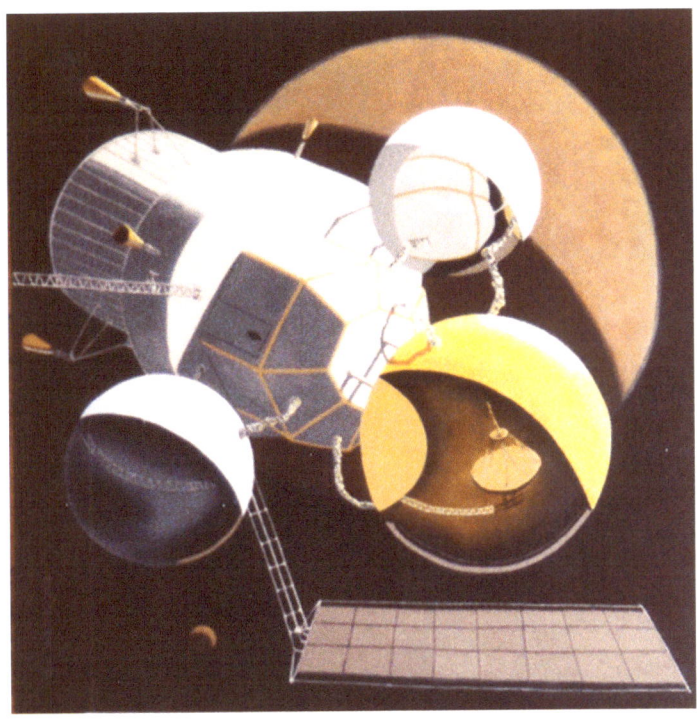

JPL Mission painting proposal — *1990* — *The Kauzlaric Art Trust*

Oil on canvas

Unfinished painting — *2007* — *The Kauzlaric Art Trust*

Oil on canvas

Missing Works

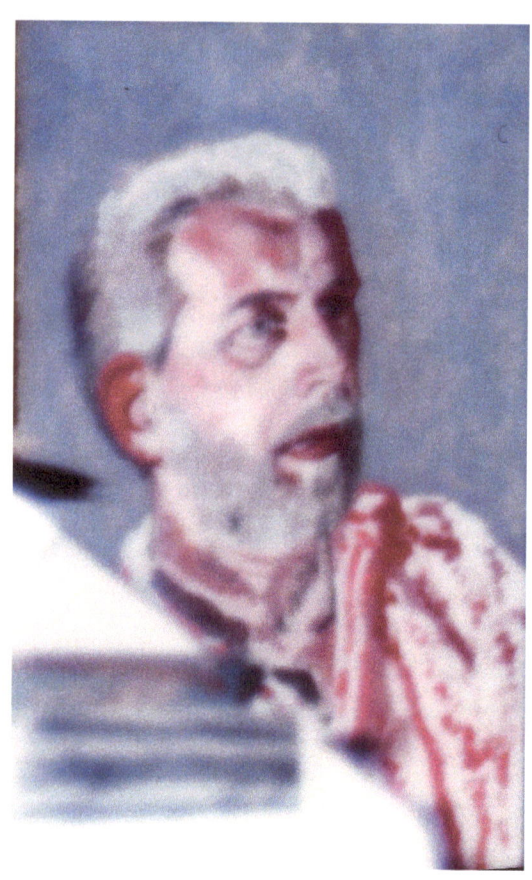

The portrait of Bruce MacKenzie (about 1979) is among the works the Kauzlaric family was unable to locate for inclusion in this book. Its last known owner was the MacKenzie family.

It is doubtful that every piece of Kauzlaric's artwork will ever be accounted for. There are several reasons for this.

First, Kauzlaric was never a meticulous record keeper. Names of paintings and transactions were sometimes hastily jotted on scraps of paper cluttering his studio. Second, he was, at best, a somewhat haphazard businessman. He sometimes sold works for a pittance because he liked somebody, or needed some quick spending money. There remains a collection of handwritten receipts and bills of sale, but these are far from consistent.

The saddest reason this visual survey isn't complete is the likely destruction of several pieces, particularly some large mosaics. Mosaics are almost always heavy, difficult to install, and built to endure the elements. Kauzlaric was proud of the engineering and design quality of his installations, claiming his mosaics would last as long as those of the Romans and Etruscans. Ironically, this sometimes was a detriment to their existence. All too often, it's easier and cheaper to destroy a mosaic than it is to dismantle or relocate it. This was the probable fate of several large mosaics that were installed at a hotel in Ocean Shores, Washington. Another mosaic fell victim to the economic meltdown of 2008, and was either destroyed or appropriated when West Sound Bank liquidated its assets.

Another mosaic, *Compass Card* (p. 209), also was a casualty of the economic downturn. The mosaic was originally purchased by then-Rainier Bank in the 1970s. The bank changed hands a couple of times and ultimately ended up a branch of local savings and loan West Sound Bank. Even after the bank closed, the mosaic was still visible in the lobby. Sadly, its whereabouts is now unknown since the building was remodeled in 2010.

There are more encouraging stories. A newspaper story about the creation of this book helped bring several works to light, including the *Ship & Compass* mosaic (p. 132) and *Fishnet* (1971, p. 136), which its current owners acquired at a flea market.

To anyone traveling in Western Washington: If you happen across a striking mosaic, a crisply lit still life, or a surrealistic painting with a hint of whimsy, check the signature. It might be a lost Kauzlaric!

Decoy & Oil Lamp — *about 1972*   *Oil on Masonite*

Missing Works

Dolphins — *1968* *Wall mosaic*

Missing Works

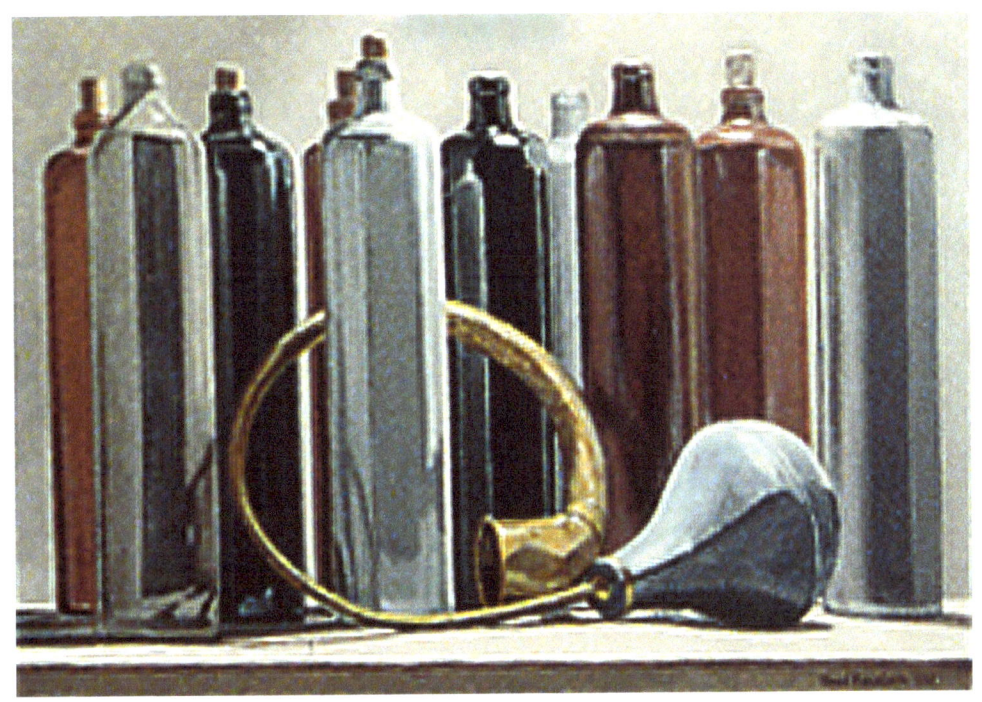

Bottles & Horn — *1982*　　　　　　　　　　　　　　　　*Oil on Masonite*

A Fish In a Coffin — *1970*　　　　　　　　　　　　　　　　*Mosaic panel*

Missing Works

Seahorse — *1965* — *Ocean Shores Inn*   *Glass and indigenous materials mosaic*

Missing Works

Seahorses — *1965 — Ocean Shores Inn* *Glass and indigenous materials*

Compass Card — *1977 — US Bank* *Glass and indigenous materials*

Lost Works

Bottles & Cultivator — *1974*　　　　　　　　　　　　　　　　　　　*Oil on Masonite*

Concrete stained glass window — 1975　　　　　　　　　*Stained glass set in cement*

Art & Kisses

An Afterword by DeAnna Kauzlaric Kieffer

In the fall of 1956, I walked in to Graham's Drive-In on Kitsap Way in Bremerton with my brother Monty. Brad Kauzlaric was seated at a large booth talking with Beth and Stu Johnson, who were mutual friends. From across the table, I noticed the oversize hand gestures almost immediately, particularly with the cigarette in hand. It was unusual for me to be "out" anywhere with my brother and even more unusual to be spoken to by his friends. Either through prompting or just to be social, my interest in art came up in conversation. "Brad is an artist, too," my brother added. Almost immediately, Brad said, "I bet I can draw better than you." These were not words that engendered warm, fuzzy feelings toward their speaker. "Really," or something equally inane was my reply.

This meeting, the gist of the conversation, and Brad's humble announcement about his abilities was something we discussed later at various times, lending credence to the how-to-win-fair-heart theories of courtship—tongue-in-cheek, of course. In time, Brad and I shared a number of sketching trips together, sometimes interrupted by stolen kisses. Eventually, he admitted that I had what he called a "fine hand" because my sketches were quick and unlabored. This speaks to the difference between us artistically. Our attitudes about

artistic talent surfaced regularly, as they were quite divergent. One thing was clear: I never shared Brad's intense dedication to art as a lifestyle and life focus—the patience and time spent in mastering techniques and sundry other requirements were his alone. To me, drawing or painting has to be fun—and fun means easy. So, I acquiesced to Brad's passion for art and his pursuit of it, knowing full well that while I was his wife, art was always his mistress.

Brad considered life an art form, and he was quite the philosopher. This shows in his designs and the subtle whimsy of much of his artwork regardless of the medium. He considered it a privilege to have his innate talent and considered it a duty to build and improve upon it. The more he faced this rigorous personal challenge, the more humble he became. Over time, the youthful gallant boast became a mature, quiet introspection. While he explored several themes over his career, his paintings were most fully realized in still life expressions and the warm surrealism of the *Channel Marker* series, as examples. "What would be, if it could be," was often his only answer when asked about the paintings intensely influenced by his many hours of rowing his Blue Heron gig on Hood Canal. While Brad enjoyed branching out into sculpture, wood carving, and concrete windows, he knew they were sometimes isolated or temporary efforts. He also knew his fervor for mosaics and oil painting was about equal, so he made an active effort to balance his time with each.

For a man whose paintings often have an otherworldly look about them, Brad was very down-to-earth and practical in most ways. He liked to garden, in part because he wanted to know how his vegetables were

Brad and DeAnna attending a dance at East High School, Bremerton, in 1956.

treated before he ate them. He had the hunter–gatherer instinct and enjoyed foraging for mushrooms such as chanterelles, oyster, morels, and the prince. He liked to pick wild red raspberries in summer, and making wine. He cut up downed trees on our property into firewood. He rarely trusted anything he couldn't eat, touch, or kick.

Brad came to Kitsap County in 1949 when his folks moved here from Minnesota. With the guidance of his Aunt Julia and Uncle Al Nelson (nephew of Ed Nelson, early Silverdale drug store proprietor), Brad and his brother Gary embarked on their personal explorations of Kitsap County and the Olympic Peninsula. They fished, hiked, biked, and camped throughout the area.

But Brad loved Seabeck the best for its beauty and its unique place in the world. Seabeck's influence on his art work is undeniable. From when he was a young man he planned to make his home in Seabeck, and he did, for 32 years.

In 1997, when the Seabeck post office moved from its waterfront location to new quarters on the Seabeck Highway, Brad converted the old building into the Seabeck Art Gallery, which he fondly described as post suburban expressions, and took pleasure in representing twenty other gifted artists there—Ken Lundemo, Ann Quinn, Carol Guthrie, and others. After two years (and repeated issues with the building's sewer system), he decided to devote more time with his own work and

DeAnna seated near Brad's easel and paints in the couple's living room at Whistle Lake Road in Anacortes, 1958

gave up the gallery. "Besides, I don't think I was cut out to be a proprietor," he told a friend.

A large chunk of Brad's life was predictable, in that he was responsible and could be depended upon to take care of what he considered to be important (although definitions do differ). We could depend on his love for us. He could be depended on at work—whether in the garbage business, or doing finish carpentry, or delivering artwork on time—and was rarely late. Friends could depend on him to do what he said he would do with few exceptions. While he may not always have done something exactly as other's might have done in similar situations, Brad took care of things as he thought best in a framework of his own established priorities. I can't recall him ever intentionally seeking to hurt or demean someone in the process. He did set a high bar and could be intolerant of those who didn't try to do their best.

Brad had no chair or lounger in the house that was "his" place to sit. Certainly, there was seating that he found comfortable, but he simply never "hung out" in any of them. Instead, he preferred to sit in the tall stool in his painting studio or to simply stand on a scrap of carpet in his mosaic shop. His natural clock was set differently than that of most people: he was both a "night owl" and an early riser. He often commented that greeting a new day was a treat, while the late-night hours filled with an eclectic range of musical favorites pouring into his studio were hand-rubbing opportunities. In his last years, he started most days with a swim at 5:30 in the morning. He had hip replacement surgery but quickly

Brad rowing his beloved Blue Heron gig on Hood Canal.

returned to his swim routine, pleased to be active again. Only three weeks before he died, he installed a new gate at the entrance to his property, cut firewood, and pruned the orchard, among other tasks. The fatigue he had begun to experience was simply post-surgical, he thought.

Time was an overriding influence in his life. It would be difficult to over-emphasize how important this influence was, and it only intensified as he grew older. At the same time, he recognized this and tried his best to mitigate it, but time could not be stopped. The day we came home from seeing his doctor, after being told his liver was cancerous, he sat in silence at the table near the garden windows. Outside, birds he fed were flitting in and away from their little feast.

I put my hand on his shoulder. He didn't move. I said I was terribly sorry but wanted him to know he could depend on me. Even though he sat there before me, I told him I was missing him already. He spoke not a word. His usual, responsive, and affable self had disappeared. He had run out of time.

Brad always knew he would never have enough of it. He often commented that if many more lifetimes were available to him, there would still be insufficient time to paint what he had in mind to paint, or build the number and variety of mosaics he wanted to build. Through his art education and artistic curiosity, he learned about or tried silkscreen, woodcarving, and stagecraft. He enjoyed them all but chose not to diffuse his pursuit of oils and mosaics. He often said he thought pottery was probably habit forming, so he never wanted to try it. "I'm certain if I put my hand to the wheel, I would be completely lost in the clay and never do anything else." If he had ever found that extra lifetime, I'm sure he would have jumped into the making of pots quite eagerly.

Brad had an interest in old clocks, especially mantle clocks, and collected a few that he struggled to keep running. Despite the best efforts of Ralph Peel, a talented, local clock repair guy, the Sessions remained a sissy and the Ansonia was temperamental. Yet, when they struck the hour in sync, which was rare, Brad felt the cacophony was a delightful mix of European bell towers. The face of an old pocket watch in his 1983 painting plays a dominate role. The Hands of Time is both factual and farce; serene and sentiment. The interplay of the gold leaf is so precise, it appears to have been applied by mechanical means. Time, again. This time made visual.

Whenever Brad's birthday rolled around, he would note how many years he had outlived his father. It seemed a matter of simple math, at first. Later, I realized he was both surprised and thankful that he had "accomplished" this feat. After his younger brother and mother died, he must have thought more often that his time was running out. Add to this the loss of other family members and friends and the reminders become more acute.

As time went by, there were activities he pursued less often or gave up entirely. Rowing his little boat simply wasn't as much fun for Brad after his friend Bruce MacKenzie died. In earlier years when practicing for a race or rowing event, he would row a triangular course that took him mid-point to Oak Head off the Toandos Peninsula in Jefferson County. Here, he would often

slip overboard and swim in the balmy summertime water of Hood Canal—a refreshing dip before rowing to Seabeck Bay and then back to the Miami Beach boat ramp. This pursuit slowly diminished. After the new century began, his Blue Heron gig sat waiting for the next row on Hood Canal, but Brad didn't get around to it.

Brad enjoyed the coffee klatches at Seabeck. They reminded him of the irascible company at Keith Bogard's Drug Store in Silverdale from his earlier days. Still, he usually didn't stay long. His focus was often so concentrated that he came across as stingy. Though we took several trips a year after I retired, I often wondered why he didn't want to take an extended trip back to Wisconsin or book a trip to Europe. His reply was, "Go if you want, go, but I choose to stay here." Why? Everything he wanted to do was in his studios. Notes, sketches, stacks of papers with designs soon to be transfigured into his latest mosaic: all this and lists of would-be titles that served as reminders of what he wanted to paint next. Time, or the idea of a lack of time, explains Brad's reluctance to do many things, as if to say, "I've but a small amount of time, so I must use it well."

When we celebrated Brad's fiftieth birthday, he wasn't happy about it at all. He had tried for some weeks to solicit a promise that no one would make a fuss. On a rainy night in February, he thought we would have a quiet evening with another couple at a dinner concert featuring Pete Barbutti. Instead, several family members and more friends showed up to share our table. Besides the German chocolate cake, Bruce MacKenzie presented Brad with a set of very dilapidated oars, saying something about using them to paddle home if the rain continued. He told me later that he was so upset at the ruse, he almost walked out. But he was later glad he hadn't. When we got home, I presented him with a gift from the family—something he had always wanted: an American-made Regulator clock.

One of the things Brad always wanted was to help his children understand the nobility of work; that to earn a living was a good thing even if the work itself wasn't particularly appealing. He said he always hoped he had left a legacy that taught his children how to work—and work effectively. If they had the ability to work at something they enjoyed and it was meaningful to them—then life simply didn't offer much better than that.

Artistic expression is a personal thing. It's a feat of derring-do to separate the personal aspects from the art. If personal stuff bumps and collides with the themes and efforts of drawings, paintings, and mosaics that Brad did over the fifty years and was part of his life, so be it. He often said I was his worst critic, and rightly so. He would be chagrined if I challenged something about his art, however minute, but if I admired a piece unabashedly, he wasn't particularly impressed. He seemed to remember what I didn't like longer than what I did. He wanted me to take an interest in what he was doing and leave him alone at the same time. He took no one's opinion of his work seriously, with the possible exception of Deloris Tarzan-Ament of *The Seattle Times*.

Being an artist, Brad would say, is to be the ultimate realist. The measure of motion (his definition of time) also fit into his faith schema. He figured time was a gift from God, but it was measured out in disproportional ways, equating it with the gift of "talents" referred to in scripture. Everyone gets the same number of hours in a day, but the number of days differs in each lifetime. It is impossible to put either your light or your talent under a bushel basket and come out ahead in the judgment game. Accountability enters into the picture, and the choices made on earth will be on some sort of scoreboard. Brad planned to have as many in the "yes" column as possible.

"To survive the act of being a lifelong artist intact is highly unlikely."

Brad Kauzlaric – 1998

ABOUT THE AUTHORS

Clayton Kauzlaric is an artist, designer, and creative director for video games. Kauzlaric studied animation and filmmaking at The Evergreen State College in Olympia, Washington, and went on to work as a designer and animator in the computer games industry. During the last twenty years, his creative work has included the highly regarded *Total Annihilation* strategy games as well as creation, design, and writing credits for the cult favorite *Voodoo Vince* for Microsoft's Xbox. Kauzlaric co-created the satirical game DeathSpank with industry legend Ron Gilbert and has designed dozens of games for smart phones, personal computers, and motion-based controllers. Kauzlaric writes and studies history, art, and music in his spare time. He lives in Bothell, Washington, near Seattle, with his wife and son.

DeAnna Kauzlaric Kieffer is a writer, graphic designer, illustrator and former director of public information at Olympic College in Bremerton, Washington. Her past work includes extensive work in publications, media management and public relations. In retirement, she devotes time to writing and illustration work. She is a graduate of the University of Washington's School of Communications. Kauzlaric Kieffer was married to Brad Kauzlaric for almost fifty years before his passing in 2007. She shares her unique insights into his life and artistic process with her contributions to this book. She now lives with husband, Robert Kieffer, near Silverdale, Washington.

Index

acrylic paints, 60

Adkisson, Harold and Virginia, 40

Alaska, 23, 28, 29

Anacortes, 24, 25, 26

Antigo, Wisconsin, 15

architectural accessories, 104

Bainbridge Island, 17-18, 23-24, 30, 49

Bainbridge Arts & Crafts, 23

Bedford, Ron, 19

Berkeley, John, 19

Billygoo Bird, 47, 190

Birkenstock sandals, 52

birthdays, 150, 215, 216

Blass, "Hank" Harrison, 20-21, 127

Blue Heron Gig, 212-213, 215

Bogard's Drug Store, 93, 215

Bosch, Hieronymus, 59

Brem-Air Disposal, 29, 34, 40, 43, 93, 149

Bremerton, 4, 16-17, 19, 21, 23, 25-27, 29-32, 36, 47, 49, 53, 149, 180, 211, 220

Brownsville, 30-31, 33, 36, 38, 54, 167

Buck, Pam and Andrew, 47

Buick Wildcat, 36

Burke Museum, 44

Byrnie Utz Hats, 52

cancer, 53, 214

Carlson, Wally, 37

Channel Marker series, 38, 48, 80, 87, 102-103, 212

Chisholm, Minnesota, 11

collectibles, 40

Colorado, Canyon City, Fort Carson, 17

Crane, Donn P., 58-59

Croatia, 8, 10, 11

Dali, Salvador, 59

devotional works, 127

Dogfish Creek, 18, 51

draft, military, 25

Eagle River, Wisconsin, 8, 12, 15, 17, 58

Floral mosaics, 45, 127

flounder, 49

Foolish Virgins, The, 112, 115, 169

Freas, Kelly, 59

Fremont, Foundry, 44

Gilberton, 31, 37, 169

Goldwater, Barry, 33

Graham's Drive-In, 22, 211

grandchildren, 11, 52

Hansville, 48

Harbor Island, 23

Harrison Memorial Hospital, 53

Hart, P.R. & Co., 29

Henrietta, 24-25

Hiz Honor John Schold, 80, 95-96, 99, 116, 169

Holbien, 59

Holy Flounder, 18, 51,

Holy Trinity Parish, 32, 149,

Hood Canal, 18, 36, 169, 212, 215,

Hoover, John, 47, 124

indigenous materials, 125

221

Japanese artists, 29
Jefferson County, 215
Johnson, Deanna, 22-26, 28-29, 30-31, 36-37, 39, 44, 46, 49, 52-53, 116, 167, 211-212, 220
Johnson, Monty, 30, 211
Jurkovich, John, 16
Kauzlaric, Alicia, 30-31, 39; Catherine, 8, 10-11, 13-17, 21, 23, 52, 59, 150; Clayton, 30-31, 39, 220 Gary; 11, 14-15, 17-18, 21-22, 51-52, 213; Jake, 8-9, 11-18, 21, 23, 34, 150; Keagan, 25-26, 30, 39; Kenton, 31; Klinton, 30-31, 39, 41; Valentine, 8-9, 12
King, Bill & Laura, 36, 43, 116, 180,
Kirkland, 26, 27
Kitsap County, 4, 6, 17-19, 29, 32, 34, 36, 42, 93, 167, 169, 213; Mall, 169; North, 23, 48; Kitsap Way, 22, 211
Kitsap Sun, 40
Lake Washington, 26, 27
landscapes, 169, 220
Lawson Gallery, 44, 46
Lone Rock, 36
Liberty Bay, 18
Lions Club, 25; Rampant, 41
Lundemo, Ken, 47, 213
Lynnwood, Washington 24
MacKenzie, Bruce, 41, 204, 215-216; Rob 41
Maplewood, 26
Marine Science Center, Poulsbo, 126
Masonite, 38,
Mata, Ann, Portrait of, 116, 119

McCormick Woods Golf Course, 19
Minnesota, 11, 213
missing Works, 204
mosaics, 125
music, 32, 180, 214
Native American, 18, 24
Nelson, Al, 17-18, 213; Julia, 18, 213
North Perry Avenue, 27, 29
Nutter, Walt, 33,
Oak Head, 215
Ocean Shores, Washington, 28-30, 127, 204
Olympic College, 19-23, 39, 43-44, 54, 63, 127, 212
Our Lady Star of the Sea Parish, 36, 149
Pacific Northwest, 3, 17, 47, 104
Penguin, Perry, The, 34
perch, 126-127, 135
politics, 33
Port Angeles, Washington, 18
portraits, 41-42, 47, 52, 63, 116, 204
Poulsbo, 17-18, 21, 51,
Poulsbo Marine Science Center, 126
Puget Sound, 6-7, 17, 24, 26, 29, 51
Quinn, Ann, 47, 213
Raphael, 60
Raski, Helen, 8
religious 59, 80, 150
Rembrandt, 59
Renton, Washington, 26, 27
retirement, 21, 80, 215

Rice, Harley and Marie, 17
rowing, 212, 215
Seabeck, 4, 18, 34, 36-38, 43- 45, 49, 53, 213, 215
Seabeck Art Gallery, 6, 46-47, 49, 52
Seabeck Elementary School, 41
Seattle, 17, 21, 23-24, 27-28, 34, 44
Seattle Art Museum, 58
Seattle Times, The, 22, 216
science fiction, 27, 59
Scorich, Mato "Matthew," 10-11; Marie, 10, 17, Catherine "Kay", 8, 10-17, 21, 23, 52, 59, 150
Schold, John, 80, 93, 95, 99, 116, 169
Schoenherr, John, 59
sculpture, 20, 38, 45, 49, 180, 212
Silverdale, 17, 39, 42, 93, 169, 213, 215
Slaughter, Mary Lou, 47
Smalley, Dean, 26
Shrimp Pot, 126
stage design, 62-63, 215
Stations of the Cross, 32, 149
Stella Maris, 45, 149, Women's Shelter, 150
Surgery, 52-53, 214
surrealism, 5, 38, 40, 42, 59, 61, 80, 104, 116, 169, 205, 212
Tarzan Ament, Deloris, 216
Teamsters, 34
Titian, 60
Toandos Peninsula, 215
tree paintings, 104, 169

Trieste, 10
unfinished Works, 191
University of Washington, 34, 44
Vermeer, 59
Walthall, Jack, 19
Wang, Arnold, 32
Western Disposal, 24, 26-27, 29, 34
Whistle Lake Road, 24,
Whitney, Ethel, 12, 59; Ray, 12-14, 59, Zola, 12-14, 58-59
Winslow, 23,
Wisconsin, 7, 8, 13, 16, 216
Witness, 150
World's Fair, 29
World War II, 19
Wyatt House, 23
Wyeth, Andrew, 58, 59

www.ingramcontent.com/pod-product-compliance
Lightning Source LLC
Chambersburg PA
CBHW040912020526
44116CB00027B/41